HIKING TEXAS
HILL COUNTRY

HELP US KEEP THIS GUIDE UP TO DATE

Every effort has been made by the author and editors to make this guide as accurate and useful as possible; however, many things can change after a guide is published—regulations change, facilities come under new management, and so forth.

We would love to hear from you concerning your experiences with this guide and how you feel it could be improved and kept up to date. While we may not be able to respond to all comments and suggestions, we'll take them to heart, and we'll also make certain to share them with the author. Please send your comments and suggestions to falconeditorial@rowman.com.

Thanks for your input!

HIKING TEXAS HILL COUNTRY

A GUIDE TO THE AREA'S GREATEST HIKING ADVENTURES

Alisha McDarris

ESSEX, CONNECTICUT

For Josh, my favorite hiking partner.

FALCONGUIDES®

An imprint of Globe Pequot, the trade division of
The Rowman & Littlefield Publishing Group, Inc.
4501 Forbes Blvd., Ste. 200
Lanham, MD 20706
www.rowman.com

Falcon and FalconGuides are registered trademarks and Make Adventure Your Story is a
trademark of The Rowman & Littlefield Publishing Group, Inc.

Distributed by NATIONAL BOOK NETWORK

British Library Cataloguing in Publication Information available

Library of Congress Cataloging-in-Publication Data

Names: McDarris, Alisha, 1987– author.
Title: Hiking Texas hill country : a guide to the area's greatest hiking adventures / Alisha McDarris.
Description: Essex, Connecticut : FalconGuides, [2024] | Includes index. | Summary: "Hiking Texas
   Hill Country will lead you down 40 of the best trails in one of the best regions of the state to
   get outdoors. Discover the rolling hills, expansive blue skies, lush vegetation, and refreshing
   creeks and streams that make Hill Country unique and the trails that take you there"—Provided
   by publisher.
Identifiers: LCCN 2023040711 (print) | LCCN 2023040712 (ebook) | ISBN 9781493072743
   (paperback) | ISBN 9781493072750 (epub)
Subjects: LCSH: Hiking—Texas—Guidebooks. | Walking—Texas—Guidebooks. | Texas—Description
   and travel. | Texas—Guidebooks.
Classification: LCC GV199.42.T49 M35 2024 (print) | LCC GV199.42.T49 (ebook) | DDC
   796.5109764—dc23/eng/20231106
LC record available at https://lccn.loc.gov/2023040711
LC ebook record available at https://lccn.loc.gov/2023040712

∞™ The paper used in this publication meets the minimum requirements of American National
Standard for Information Sciences—Permanence of Paper for Printed Library Materials, ANSI/
NISO Z39.48-1992.

CONTENTS

THE HIKES

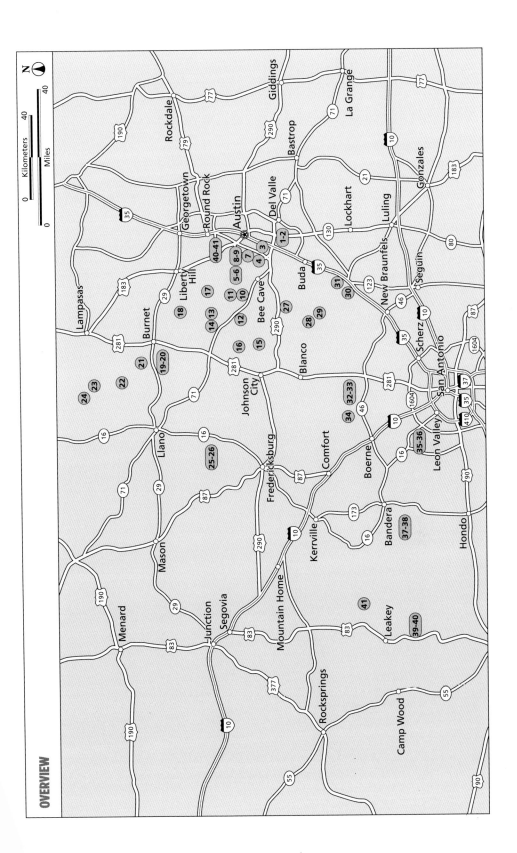

ACKNOWLEDGMENTS

A big, fat, snack-fueled thanks to my husband, Josh, for accompanying me on many of these hikes that frequently took longer than I initially promised, and for (almost) never complaining when I wanted to squeeze in a few more miles before sunset or stop to take the 117th photo. I also must raise a glass to Jo, who not only kept up with my ridiculous pace on several of these routes, but also provided the cocktail fixings for après hike drinks on several occasions. A heartfelt thanks to friend and fellow guidebook writer Adam who encouraged me to join the Falcon family and to all the brilliant editors who helped transform a manuscript into a coherent and beautiful book. Thanks, too, Mom and Dad, for introducing me to the wonders of the great outdoors. I'll be forever grateful.

The colorful 360-degree views from Decision Point at Reveille Peak Ranch are best enjoyed just before sunset.

MEET YOUR GUIDE

Alisha McDarris is a travel and outdoor journalist, passionate outdoorist, and co-founder of the sustainable outdoor adventure blog and YouTube channel terradrift.com where she and her husband, Josh, produce gear guides, how-tos, trip reports, and more to help more people get outside more often and do so responsibly and sustainably. She's been backpacking since she was 10 and hiking since she could walk. She lived in Austin for eight years, spending much of that time exploring the trails and parks unique to central Texas. Frequently nomadic, she loves to adventure in parks and wilderness areas around the world, but Hill Country will always have a soft spot in her heart.

Afternoon sunlight streams through the trees at Wild Basin Wilderness Preserve.

INTRODUCTION

WELCOME TO HILL COUNTRY

Located just off-center in the largest state in the contiguous United States, between the flat plains of west Texas and the towering pines and humid swamps of southeast Texas, Hill Country beckons. In the some 31,000 square miles or so that make up the region, rolling hills and limestone cliffs, granite escarpments and underground reservoirs, flowing rivers and abundant wildflowers bask under skies so wide and blue, darkness so steeped in stars that "Big Sky Country" seems a more apt slogan than "The Lone Star State."

It's unique among Texas landscapes. Perched atop the Edwards Plateau, an aquifer buried deep below the limestone the region is famous for, creeks, rivers, and natural springs bubble up and bring life to a diverse array of plants and wildlife, some of which can be found nowhere else on Earth: the golden-cheeked warbler, Texas blind salamander, and Texas snowbells, to name a few.

Winding roads that rise and fall in picturesque undulations lead to beloved trailheads and paths that curve around sunny lakes or zigzag through open prairies or scale course granite domes and layered limestone escarpments. Here, a variety of landscapes feature a range of types of hiking trails, from sunny and flat to steep and challenging. In short, there's plenty to explore.

That said, hiking opportunities tend to be spread out in Hill Country, largely because over 95 percent of the land in Texas is privately owned, meaning there are fewer recreation opportunities on public land than those familiar with hiking in the American West might expect. But it's hard to be disappointed when crushed granite or packed dirt paths lead you to vernal pools, cobalt swimming holes, to overlooks with expansive views, and alongside evergreen cedar breaks and vibrant wildflowers.

It's these views and landscapes that captured my heart after moving to the region. And every new trail I discovered I wanted to share with others. This guidebook describes many of them, both widely beloved and underrated hiking opportunities in a region I called home for more of my adult life than anywhere else thus far.

LAND ACKNOWLEDGMENT

This book is intended to help you explore and experience the wonders of Hill Country, and we respectfully acknowledge that this book highlights the traditional lands of many Native Peoples, especially the Apache, Comanche, Tonkawa, Kiowa, Kickapoo, and Coahuiltecan, who once and still call the region home.

WEATHER

Summers in Hill Country, much like the rest of Texas, can get brutally hot. It's not uncommon to see highs up to 110°F June through September, though temperatures closer to 100°F are more common. Once the sun sets, temperatures are often more bearable, but frequently still humid. On the upside, the region rarely gets snow or sees frigid temperatures, which makes hiking year-round a welcome possibility. Rain tends to be intermittent and unpredictable, but most often occurs in the spring. Fall is a very popular time for hiking in central Texas when temperatures drop and campgrounds are full to capacity. For up-to-date weather forecasts and conditions, check the National Weather Service before you hit the trail.

LOCAL PLANTS AND ANIMALS

There's much unique flora and fauna to appreciate in Hill Country, from the ubiquitous Ashe juniper, prickly pear cactus, live oak, and nine-banded armadillo to the iconic bluebonnets and wildflowers that bloom in spring, the black-capped vireo that was recently removed from the threatened species list, and Texas wild rice.

The golden-cheeked warbler only nests in juniper trees in Hill Country in the spring and summer—nowhere else in the world—cypress trees and maples paint the landscapes yellow and red in the fall, and swaying native grasses, deer and rabbits, and twisted madrone trees all populate area topography. You may even get to see a wild hog or watch bats dive from above for their dinner.

SNAKE ETIQUETTE

When hiking in Hill Country, you may come across a venomous snake from time to time. Fear not! They don't want any more to do with you than you do with them. But stay safe by keeping your distance—at least 10 to 15 feet is a good rule of thumb—and don't try to antagonize or encourage them to move off the trail. Either go around, giving them a wider berth than you think is necessary, or stand back and wait for them to move along. And in the extremely unlikely event that you are bitten, don't bother with any of the "remedies" you may have heard about; the only way to treat a venomous snakebite is with anti-venom, so head to the hospital immediately for appropriate medical care.

WILDERNESS RESTRICTIONS/REGULATIONS

Texas is comprised almost entirely of privately owned land. That means throughout Hill Country and beyond, there is little to no wilderness to speak of and almost every hike in the state, including in Hill Country, is in a state, county, city, or privately operated park. So pay close attention to hours of operation and fee requirements before you arrive at your intended hiking destination.

DISABILITY ACCESS

Most of the trails in this book are not accessible to people using a wheelchair. Those that are will be identified.

HOW TO USE THIS GUIDE

In each hike description, you'll find the same headings with helpful info to assist you in planning and executing your hike. Here's what each one is for.

Start: This is a short summary of the starting location for the hike to help you figure out where to set foot on trail.

Elevation gain: To help determine a hike's difficulty, check the elevation gain, which is listed as the highest and lowest point on the trail. But don't assume these numbers indicate one long climb or descent. On the contrary, in Hill Country, you'll often find yourself hiking up, then down, then up again, which means there may be more elevation gain than the high and low points indicate.

Fortunately, absolute elevation isn't an issue in Hill Country; peaks here don't get high enough for oxygen concentrations to wane.

Distance: The distance specified in each description is listed as a round-trip distance from the trailhead and back, encompassing the entire route be it an out-and-back, loop, or anything in between.

Hike lengths have been estimated as closely as possible using topographic maps, park maps, and GPS tracking. Distances may vary by a few tenths of a mile as a result.

Difficulty: Assessing a hike's difficulty is subjective. The elevation, elevation change, and length all play a role, as do trail condition, weather, and a hiker's physical condition. However, I've categorized each hike based on what a moderately active adult may be capable of without much difficulty. That said, many hikes may be rated more difficult not because of elevation gain, but time spent in direct sunlight, which could make a hike more strenuous in the summer months. Extremely rocky trails may also bump the rating if you have to be more aware of your footing. Likewise, a hike that takes 4 hours instead of one will be rated more difficult simply because of the time and stamina required.

Hiking time: The hiking time is a rough estimate of the amount of time the average hiker will take to complete the hike. If you're in excellent shape, you may be able to complete it in less time. If you like to take it slow or require more time to rest between climbs, it may take a bit longer. I based the estimated time on a few factors, including how long it took me (a fast, sure-footed hiker, but one who makes frequent stops to take photos) to complete the hike, plus estimates from park maps and apps, which tend to offer longer estimates.

Seasons/schedule: The season specified for a hike is the optimum or ideal season to hit that particular trail. Since snow falls rarely, winter is almost never off limits for hiking in Central Texas, meaning all the trails in this guide can be hiked any time of year. However, given the merciless temperatures in the summer, spring and fall are often offered as the best seasons for hiking, particularly on exposed trails. But if summer is when you like to hike, simply hit the trail in the early morning to beat the hottest part of the day and bring plenty of water.

As for what season is objectively best, they all offer something unique. Spring brings pleasant temperatures and wildflowers, but occasionally more rain. Summer is a great time to explore trails with swimming holes, but is often very hot. Several areas of Hill Country feature a vibrant show of colors in the fall and are extremely popular that time of year. And winter often means more secluded trails and still plenty of greenery in the form of evergreen plants like cacti and juniper.

Some hiking areas do have opening or closing times, like state parks, which close their gates unless you have a camping reservation, so if you're planning on hiking very early or very late, check before you go.

Fees and permits: Permits are not usually required to day hike in Hill Country, but many areas require an entry fee. I highly recommend a Texas State Parks Pass if you plan to visit more than a few parks, especially if you're traveling as a family (the pass covers everyone in your vehicle) or you want to camp (the pass offers camping discounts in addition to admission to every state park for a full year).

When visiting country or private parks, be prepared with cash; many don't take credit cards or checks.

Trail contacts: The trail contacts section lists the name, address, website, and phone number of the managing agency for the lands through which the trail passes. Call, write, or check the website for current information about the hike like trail closures or to make a reservation.

Canine compatibility: This section describes whether dogs are allowed on the trail. Generally, dogs need to be leashed when they are allowed, but a few hikes permit off-leash dogs. Please be courteous and always pick up after your dog.

Trail surface: Trail surface describes the material the trail is made of. Often in Hill Country, that will be dirt or rock (limestone or granite are in abundance depending on what part of Hill Country you're in).

Land status: This simply explains which agency—usually state or privately owned—manages the land over which the trail passes. In this book, it's most often Texas Parks and Wildlife Department and County Parks.

Nearest town: The nearest town is the closest city or town to the hike's trailhead that has at least basic visitor services like gas, food, or lodging. Keep in mind that the smaller the town, the more limited the hours of operation are likely to be.

Other trail users: This describes the other users that you might encounter on the hike. Mountain bikers and equestrians are the most common.

Maps: The maps in this guide are as accurate and current as possible and when used in conjunction with the hike description and the additional maps listed for each hike, you should have little trouble following the route.

State parks and natural areas have fantastic park and trail maps available for free at entrance stations, but privately owned parks and trails may have less detailed information.

USGS maps may also be available for many areas highlighted in this book, but as they aren't updated often, privately owned trail systems may not me mapped. When they are, though, USGS topographic quadrangles are generally the most detailed and accurate maps available, especially when it comes to natural features and landscapes. That said, the hikes in this guide do not require a supremely detailed topo map. If you wish to purchase one anyway, they're usually available at outdoor stores or directly from USGS at http://store.usgs.gov. Simply find the state, the number or city of your desired map, or search for the exact map name listed in the hike heading.

GPS (Global Positioning System) units and apps, particularly those with installed or downloadable maps, can be extremely useful for route finding when used in conjunction with paper maps, especially on poorly marked routes.

Water availability: Check this section to find out whether water is available at, or near, the trailhead. If it isn't, make sure to arrive prepared with plenty for your hike.

Special considerations: If there are unique elements of a trail that require extra preparation or advance planning, they will be listed here, including notes about heat, sun exposure, or if reservations are required.

Amenities available: This section will share what necessities are available near the trailhead like restrooms, running water, shelter, ramps, etc.

Maximum grade: Trail grade is a good indication of how hard the hardest part of the hike gets. It will tell you how steep the trail gets and how long the steepest section lasts.

Cell service: This section tells you whether you can or cannot expect cell service along the route. If there isn't any, don't rely on it for communication or navigation. Remember that different carriers sometimes have different coverage areas.

Finding the trailhead: Here you'll find detailed directions to the trailhead. With a basic current road map or GPS app, you can easily locate the starting point from the directions, with or without coordinates. In general, a main road you'll be using to approach the trailhead is used as the starting point.

Distances may vary slightly in their measurements, so be sure to keep an eye out for signs, junctions, and landmarks mentioned in the directions. These will also help in the case you don't have cell service or GPS directions are slightly off.

All of the hikes in this guide have trailheads that are accessible with any type of vehicle with any type of clearance.

Trail conditions: Trails in Hill Country vary. Some will be wide, others narrow, some rocky, others smooth, some flat, others rolling. And the type of trail surface and condition may change over the course of the hike. So this section will address what to expect.

The Hike: All of the hikes selected for this guide can be done easily by people in good physical condition. Some may require some scrambling, others low creek crossings, but none require any special equipment or skills.

The trails are typically marked with blazes, metal directional markers, signposts, or sometimes rock cairns (small piles of rocks built along the trail to indicate direction when hiking on smooth rock surfaces). Most of the time, paths are obvious and easy to follow, but the blazes and directions help when multiple trails intersect or when paths are faint or overgrown.

The description of the hike is also intended to help you select a hike that appeals to you so you can get out there and enjoy.

Miles and Directions: To help you stay on course, this section lists mileages between significant landmarks or junctions along the trail.

MAP LEGEND

Municipal
≡⟨10⟩≡ Interstate Highway
≡⟨290⟩≡ US Highway
≡⟨173⟩≡ State Road
━━━━━ Local Road
= = = = Gravel Road

Trails
∎∎∎∎∎∎ Featured Trail
- - - - - - Trail

Water Features
⬭ Body of Water
∿ River/Creek
ơ Spring
≋ Waterfall
∥ Rapids

Symbols
‿ Bridge
▪ Building/Point of Interest
Ⓐ Campground
⥮ Gate
🅿 Parking
▲ Peak
▲ Primitive Campground
🚻 Restrooms
🔰 Scenic View/Overlook
⦀ Stairs
○ Town
① Trailhead
❓ Visitor/Information Center

Land Management
▢ Park/Preserve/Natural Area

1 MCKINNEY FALLS STATE PARK HOMESTEAD TRAIL

This mostly flat, easy trail offers a leisurely and shady stroll through lush greenery and a lively swimming hole surrounded by limestone cliffs and towering cypress trees. In warmer months, the falls at the start and end of the hike are extremely popular with water lovers who enjoy leaping from the top of the low falls into the refreshing water below, but the farther reaches of the trail aren't quite as crowded and offer a peaceful respite in natural surroundings.

Start: Homestead Trail Trailhead
Elevation gain: 476 to 594 feet
Distance: 3.3-mile loop
Difficulty: Easy
Hiking time: 1.5 hours
Seasons/schedule: Year-round, open 8 a.m.–10 p.m.
Fees and permits: $6 per person
Trail contacts: McKinney Falls State Park, 5808 McKinney Falls Parkway, Austin, TX 78744; (512) 243-1643; https://tpwd.texas.gov/state-parks/mckinney-falls/#
Canine compatibility: On-leash only
Trail surface: Dirt, rock
Land status: Texas Parks and Wildlife
Nearest town: Austin
Other trail users: Hikers, mountain bikers
Maps: TPWD maps: https://tpwd.texas.gov/state-parks/mckinney-falls/map
Water availability: Yes, at entrance station and bathrooms, not at trailhead
Special considerations: After heavy rains, consult the park before hiking this trail as a flooded creek can make crossing dangerous.
Amenities available: Restrooms, picnic tables, shelters, and playground down the park road from the trailhead
Maximum grade: 10% for 0.2 miles
Cell service: Available throughout

FINDING THE TRAILHEAD

From the entrance gate, drive down the main road and take the first right toward Lower Falls. Follow the road until it dead-ends at the parking area. The trailhead begins where the road dead-ends in a cul-de-sac. **GPS:** 30.186195, -97.721325

Trail conditions: Most of the trail is narrow and composed of packed dirt, which can get muddy after rain. There are several rocky sections and a portion of the trail that involves walking over a smooth limestone field. In times of high water, be prepared to get your feet wet as you cross Onion Creek.

THE HIKE

Just a 15-minute drive from downtown Austin is one of the area's most popular parks for hiking, picnicking, and swimming: McKinney Falls State Park. And while many argue that it's located outside of the technical boundaries of Hill Country proper, the Homestead Trail still offers an opportunity to take a walk through the type of historical and natural beauty often found in the region, including architecture from the 1800s and a variety of plant and animal life (not to mention wildflowers in the spring and several swimmable waterfalls).

The falls at the start and end of the trail.

To start exploring, follow the sign that points straight down a wide, uneven, dirt and rock-strewn path that soon gives way to a wide bed of limestone surrounded by Ashe juniper, live oak, and black willow. Traverse the limestone field and cross Onion Creek above the falls, treading carefully between the sculpted rock that's been carved out by moving water over thousands of years. It's often slippery and tricky to cross, so take extra care and consider bringing sandals to keep your hiking shoes dry.

Much of the narrow path is shaded.

Or, on a hot day, indulge in a swim. There's at least some water flowing over the falls year-round, but there's no lifeguard on duty, so swim at your own risk. And check with park staff beforehand as bacteria levels or dangerous conditions occasionally make the water off-limits.

Once you cross the creek, at about 0.3 miles, a sign on your left points toward the Homestead Trail, a narrow dirt path that heads into the trees. Take it, and bask in the narrow, winding, and largely shaded route through the woods. Smooth curving branches of Texas persimmon point the way, and in spring and summer, inland wild oats, roundleaf greenbriar, and tall grasses grow close against the trail and abundant foliage overhead pro-

> On weekends or holidays it's highly recommended that you make a day-use reservation online as the park will fill up quickly and close the gates to new visitors.

vides ample shade. But as you progress, enjoy the view as plant life changes around you, from deciduous trees to narrow-trunked cedar elms to dense pockets of Ashe juniper, to fields of wildflowers.

At about 0.4 miles, you will reach what's left of the fenced-off stone block McKinney Homestead that once belonged to Thomas McKinney. Keep the fence and the homestead on your right as you continue down the path and back into the woods.

Around 1.2 miles, a three-way junction near the old homestead offers a shortcut back to the trailhead, but continue on Homestead Trail, which curves gently to the left.

Then, near 2.1 miles, you will reach the junction with the Flint Rock Loop Trail. Taking this trail to the left tacks on a few extra miles to your hike via a couple of additional loops, but to stay on Homestead Trail, continue straight.

Over the ages, flowing water has carved unique shapes in the limestone along the creek.

What remains of the old McKinney Homestead, the trail's namesake.

As you near the end of the journey, keep an eye out for wildflowers and prickly pear cactus that bloom in the spring as the wooded trail opens up. You'll soon reach the Gristmill Spur Trail and the remains of the McKinney Grist Mill, one of the first flour mills in the area that took advantage of the flow of Onion Creek to power the machinery.

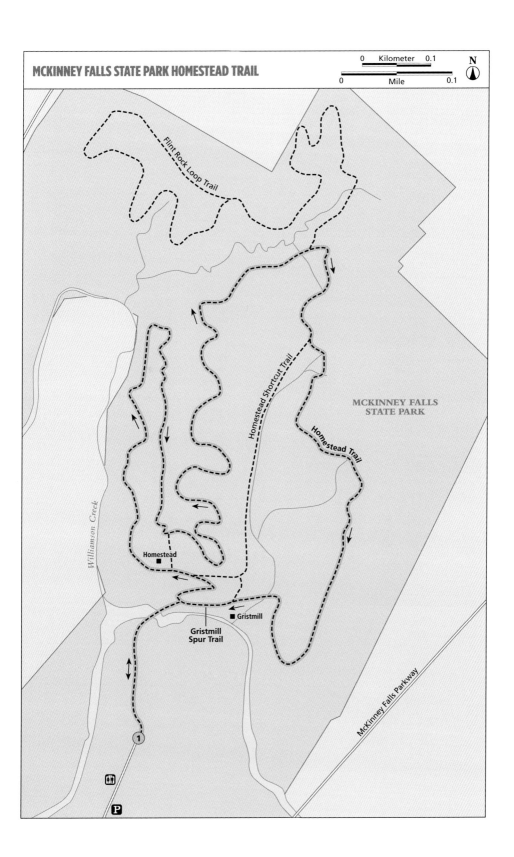

MCKINNEY FALLS STATE PARK HOMESTEAD TRAIL

0   Kilometer   0.1

0   Mile   0.1

N

Flint Rock Loop Trail

Homestead Shortcut Trail

MCKINNEY FALLS
STATE PARK

Homestead Trail

Williamson Creek

■ Homestead

■ Gristmill

Gristmill
Spur Trail

1

McKinney Falls Parkway

P

Wildflowers line sections of the trail in spring.

Immediately after you pass the mill, the trail spits you back out on the limestone bed around the falls. From here, hike back across the creek the way you came and retrace your steps to the parking lot.

MILES AND DIRECTIONS

0.0 Start at the Homestead Trail Trailhead off the Lower Falls parking lot.

0.2 Cross the limestone bed and Onion Creek above the falls.

0.3 Turn left following signs for the Homestead Trail.

0.4 Reach the homestead. Take the trail to the left, keeping the fence and homestead on your right.

1.2 Continue straight at the junction to stay on Homestead Trail.

2.1 At the junction with Flint Rock Loop, continue straight to stay on Homestead Trail.

2.2 Continue on Homestead Trail past the Homestead Shortcut.

3.0 Veer left to head toward the parking lot on the Gristmill Spur Trail, following the trail marker with a P. In a few feet, pass the remains of the McKinney Grist Mill.

3.1 Return to the beginning of the loop. Retrace your steps across the Lower Falls to the parking lot.

3.3 Arrive back at the trailhead.

2 MCKINNEY FALLS STATE PARK ONION CREEK TRAIL

This paved, often shady, and tree-lined trail winds through woods, past picnic tables, and alongside Onion Creek. While it may not offer much in the way of elevation gain or epic views, it's an easy, improved-surface trail perfect for families, friends, even bikes and all-terrain wheelchairs.

Start: Onion Creek Hike and Bike Trailhead
Elevation gain: 489 to 623 feet
Distance: 2.9-mile loop
Difficulty: Easy due to paved path and only one section of gradual elevation change
Hiking time: 1.5 hours
Seasons/schedule: Year-round, open 8 a.m.–10 p.m.
Fees and permits: $6 per person
Trail contacts: McKinney Falls State Park, 5808 McKinney Falls Parkway, Austin, TX 78744; (512) 243-1643; https://tpwd.texas.gov/state-parks/mckinney-falls/#
Canine compatibility: On-leash only
Trail surface: Asphalt

Land status: Texas Parks and Wildlife
Nearest town: Austin
Other trail users: Hikers, bikers
Maps: TPWD maps: https://tpwd.texas.gov/state-parks/mckinney-falls/map
Water availability: At the Smith Visitor Center near the trailhead
Special considerations: The park has a GRIT all-terrain wheelchair available to the public during office hours (daily 8 a.m.–5 p.m.). Email or call to reserve the chair for your visit.
Amenities available: Restrooms, picnic tables, charcoal grills, education and information center
Maximum grade: 8% for 0.4 miles
Cell service: Throughout

FINDING THE TRAILHEAD

From the park entrance, drive down the park road, following signs for the Upper Falls. The trailhead is located at the end of the parking lot. **GPS:** 30.183844, -97.725612

Trail conditions: The entirety of the trail is paved, though uneven in spots, except for a brief gravel section at the start of the hike that leads down to the falls.

THE HIKE

If it's a leisurely, shaded, improved surface trail you're in the mood for with plenty of places to set up a picnic or take a dip in the falls, this one will do the trick. Between plenty of tree cover, creek access, and a path wide enough for at least two, it's an easy and delightful stroll. In the early spring a field of bluebonnets blooms across from the trailhead parking lot and in the summer there's an abundance of greenery.

> On weekends or holidays it's highly recommended that you make a day-use reservation online as the park will fill up quickly and close gates to new visitors.

But the best part of the journey may be the beginning and end, where the Upper Falls beckons swimmers just down the short hill from the trailhead. It's a beloved attraction

A view of the falls and swimming hole near the start of the trail.

among park visitors who lounge on the banks among limestone cliffs, tall grasses, and majestic bald cypress trees all summer long.

Whether or not you enjoy a soak, follow the paved Onion Creek Trail as it curves to the left, away from the falls. You will spend 0.5 miles or so walking through a large, grassy picnic area with dozens of picnic tables, charcoal grills, and several water spigots, all shaded by mature live oak trees. Several dirt footpaths lead down to the creek, as do a few paths that lead to other parking areas along the park road.

Around 0.6 miles, you'll leave the picnic area and the paved trail will continue to be mostly shaded and green thanks to live oaks, vines, and native grasses. There's also poison ivy, though, so stay on the trail. At a few points along the way, the forest will open up to small clearings dotted with juniper, prickly pear cactus, Texas persimmon, and Christmas cholla cactus.

When you reach the junction at 1.9 miles, head to the right to stay on Onion Creek Trail; continuing straight will lead you to the campground. When you reach the park road, cross and continue straight. As soon as you do, you'll see on your right the remains of a stone horse trainer's cabin built in the early 1850s for the park's namesake's horse trainer John Van Hagan.

After you pass the ruins of the structure, at 2.8 miles, continue on Onion Creek Trail as it curves to the left, past the junction with the picnic trail. In another moment, cross the park road again and you'll see the visitor center on the right. Inside there is abundant

Cypress trees grow along the pools near the falls.

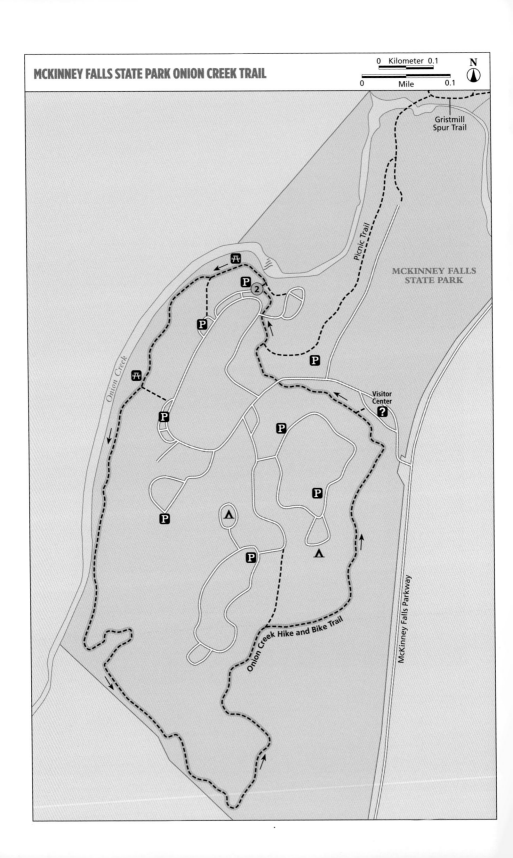

MCKINNEY FALLS STATE PARK ONION CREEK TRAIL

0   Kilometer   0.1

0   Mile   0.1

N

Gristmill
Spur Trail

Picnic Trail

MCKINNEY FALLS
STATE PARK

Onion Creek

Visitor
Center
?

McKinney Falls Parkway

Onion Creek Hike and Bike Trail

The picturesque limestone beds surrounding the falls.

information about the park, its history and ecology, plus a viewing deck where you can peer down at the falls. But to complete the hike, continue straight across the road on the paved path that curves back toward the trailhead parking lot.

MILES AND DIRECTIONS

- **0.0** Start from the Onion Creek Hike and Bike Trailhead and descend toward the falls, keeping them on your right.
- **0.4** Pass a gravel trail on your left that leads up to another parking area. Continue straight.
- **1.9** At the junction, head right to stay on Onion Creek Trail.
- **2.7** Cross the park road and continue straight onto Onion Creek Trail.
- **2.8** At the junction that leads to the Lower Falls, veer left to stay on Onion Creek Trail.
- **2.9** Arrive back at the trailhead parking lot.

3 VIOLET CROWN TRAIL: ZILKER PARK TO 360

Lots of shade, swimming holes, abundant creek crossings, and plenty of unique limestone formations make this trail exceedingly popular with locals and visitors. On pleasant weekends, especially when the creek is flowing, expect an abundance of visitors and a full parking lot (don't worry, there's plenty of parking around sprawling Zilker Park), but on weekdays, thin crowds offer a peaceful escape. Bring sandals during wet seasons to aid in multiple creek crossings.

Start: Zilker Park Trailhead
Elevation gain: 449 to 538 feet
Distance: 7.2-mile out-and-back
Difficulty: Easy due to mostly flat trails with only slight, brief elevation change
Hiking time: 3.5 hours
Seasons/schedule: Year-round, most pleasant in the spring and fall
Fees and permits: None, but there is a fee for parking
Trail contacts: Austin Parks and Recreation, 200 S. Lamar Blvd., Austin, TX 78704; (512) 974-6700; https://www.austintexas.gov/department/parks-and-recreation
Canine compatibility: On-leash only
Trail surface: Dirt, rock
Land status: City park
Nearest town: Austin

Other trail users: Mountain bikers, rock climbers
Maps: Austin Parks and Recreation, Violet Crown Trail, https://violetcrowntrail.com/wp-content/uploads/2016/01/VCT_ZilkerTo360_pdf.pdf, https://www.austintexas.gov/sites/default/files/files/Parks/GIS/Barton_Creek_GBelt_Web_Map_reduced.pdf
Water availability: Yes, at the bathrooms
Special considerations: Some sections of the trail are in full sun and can be hot in the summer.
Amenities available: Bathrooms, water, picnic tables and shelters in nearby Zilker Park
Maximum grade: 10% for 0.1 miles
Cell service: Throughout

FINDING THE TRAILHEAD

From Barton Springs Road, turn onto William Barton Drive and follow signs for Barton Springs Pool. The trailhead is located at the far southwest end of the pool parking lot. **GPS:** 30.264126, -97.773284

Trail conditions: The trail is a combination of narrow dirt paths, rocky trails, and involves a few creek crossings. Much of the trail is in partial shade, but there are several sections in full sun. During wet seasons, swimming holes abound.

THE HIKE

The Violet Crown Trail, based on a nickname given to the city in the late 1800s believed to be a reference to the violet-hued sunsets the city enjoys, is yet another peaceful urban escape within Austin's city limits.

Lined with live oak, native grasses, and wildflowers in the spring, when complete, the trail will be 30 miles long (as of this writing it has reached 13), but this portion that overlaps with the Barton Creek Greenbelt Trail may be the most easily accessible with trailhead parking lots at both ends and no sidewalk sections. Plus, during seasons with

Wildflowers along the trail.

heavy precipitation (often spring and fall), you'll have access to the many swimming holes along Barton Creek.

Start at the Zilker Park Trailhead next to Barton Springs Pool. A fairly wide crushed gravel path, flat and sunny, marked with a map and trail info, signals the start.

In short order, the trail will turn from crushed gravel to a dirt path and soon become the familiar rock-strewn landscape of Hill Country. Several side trails, some of which connect to Barton Creek, will fork off to the left and the right throughout the trail, but stay on the main path.

As you near the half-mile mark, large limestone cliffs rise up on your right, the creek on your left. The creek, fed by the Edwards Aquifer, is frequently dry during seasons of little to no rain, which makes for easy, dry crossings for much of the year. But if it's cooling streams and swimming holes you want, your best chance is to hike in the spring or after seasonal rains. During these times, locals flock to the many swimming holes along this section of trail, one of which is located at the 0.8-mile mark.

On trail, much of your hike will be partially shaded by live oak, juniper, and American sycamore, including around picturesque side trails (worth the short detour) like to Campbell's Hole and Flat Rocks where shady groves offer a place to sit and rest after climbing over the large boulders and rock formations.

You'll cross the creek bed from time to time, which is often dry, rocky, and alive with plant life like giant ragweed and snow on the mountain, delicate white flowers that bloom from green and white leaves.

At 2.2 miles, you'll pass beneath Gus Fruh, a high limestone wall very popular with climbers. Take the narrow path just below the climbing wall and you will see a trail marker ahead. Here, keep left to continue on the main trail. After this point, you'll likely have more of the path and its lovely sections of dense Ashe juniper forest where the trees' shaggy trunks bend over the trail to yourself.

A partially shaded, rocky path.

When you reach the junction with the 360 Trailhead (you'll know it by its stone steps), you may continue straight to keep going on the Violet Crown or Greenbelt Trail, or you can sit, rest, have a snack, and turn around and retrace your steps.

Limestone cliffs flank a portion of the trail.

On your way back, make sure to veer right on the alternate route at 6.0 miles to check out Flat Rocks for fun photo ops of the unique geological zone if you didn't investigate on the first pass. The trail will meet back up with the Campbell's Hole side trail and then the main trail.

> After your hike, cool off with a dip in Barton Springs Pool, a stunning natural, spring-fed pool that's 68ºF year-round and offers exceptional views of the city skyline.

MILES AND DIRECTIONS

- **0.0** Start from Zilker Trailhead.
- **0.8** Arrive at a swimming hole with rope swings.
- **0.9** Take the trail to the left to Campbell's Hole.
- **1.0** Veer left when the Campbell's Hole trail meets back up with the main trail.
- **1.2** Continue straight at the junction with the side trail to the Flats. Continue straight at the junction with the Spyglass Trailhead.
- **1.5** Cross over a rocky creek bed.
- **1.6** Veer left to stay on the main trail, following the signs on the trail markers.
- **1.9** At the fork, veer right and cross the creek bed. Turn left as soon as you cross to stay on the main trail.

Juniper branches bend over the trail.

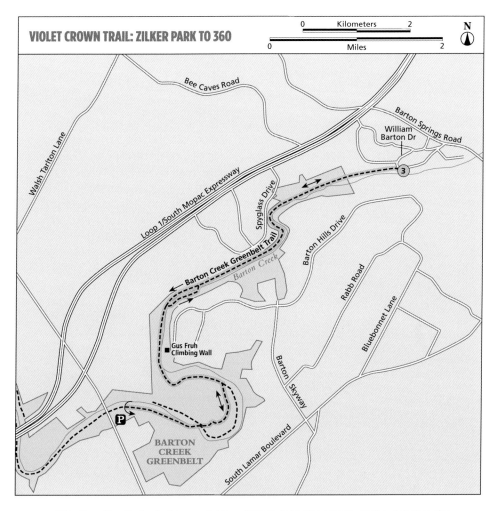

0   Kilometers   2

0   Miles   2

N

2.2   Pass Gus Fruh climbing wall. Veer right to take the narrow path just below the climbing wall. At the trail marker, bear left to stay on the main trail.

2.3   Continue on the main trail that curves right at the junction with the Gus Fruh Trailhead trail.

2.4   Turn left to stay on the main trail and cross the creek bed.

2.6   Continue straight on the wide path.

2.8   Continue on the unobstructed path that curves to the right.

3.1   At the Y-junction, follow the main trail as it curves to the left and cross the creek bed. After you cross, turn right onto the main trail following the trail marker.

3.4   At the junction, take the trail on the right. At the Violet Crown Trail marker, turn right.

3.6   Reach the junction with the 360 Trailhead. Turn around and retrace your steps.

6.0   At the junction with the Flat Rocks side trail, turn right.

6.2   Rejoin the Campbell's Hole side trail.

6.3   Rejoin the main trail.

7.2   Arrive back at the trailhead.

4 BARTON CREEK GREENBELT: HILL OF LIFE FALLS TO TWIN FALLS

Spread over more than 800 acres, Barton Creek Greenbelt is beloved by locals and visitors alike for a reason. There's an abundant variety of plant life, plenty of opportunities to cool off in a number of swimming holes during wetter seasons, and the trail offers a delightful, easy wander through a picturesque and often shaded landscape that meanders alongside the water. Though there are more than 12 miles of trails along the Greenbelt, this section features the highest concentration of small waterfalls and interesting rock structures.

Start: Trail's End Access to Barton Creek Trail, also known as Hill of Life Trailhead
Elevation gain: 575 to 883 feet
Distance: 5.7-mile out-and-back
Difficulty: Moderate due to a steep section at the beginning and end
Hiking time: 3 hours
Seasons/schedule: Year-round but most pleasant in the spring and fall or when water is high
Fees and permits: None
Trail contacts: Austin Parks and Recreation, 200 S. Lamar Blvd., Austin, TX 78704; (512) 974-6700; https://www.austintexas.gov/department/parks-and-recreation
Canine compatibility: On-leash only

Trail surface: Dirt, rock
Land status: City park
Nearest town: Austin
Other trail users: Mountain bikes, rock climbers
Maps: Austin Parks and Recreation, https://www.austintexas.gov/sites/default/files/files/Parks/GIS/Barton_Creek_GBelt_Web_Map_reduced.pdf
Water availability: None
Special considerations: There's no parking lot at this trailhead, only street parking, which is metered on the blocks surrounding the trailhead.
Amenities available: None, so come prepared
Maximum grade: 15% for 0.5 miles
Cell service: Throughout

FINDING THE TRAILHEAD

 From S. Capital of Texas Highway (or Loop 360) turn onto Scottish Woods Trail. Park near the top of the hill where the road dead-ends into Camp Craft Road. Turn right onto Camp Craft Road to reach the trailhead, which is on a residential street. An informational sign with a map marks the trailhead.
GPS: 30.275159, -97.825238

Trail conditions: The trail is a combination of narrow dirt paths, rocky trails, and a fairly steep section of gravel and limestone at the start and end. Much of the trail is in partial shade, but there are several sections in full sun. During wet seasons, swimming holes abound.

THE HIKE

Popular with hikers, mountain bikers, families, and dogs, Barton Creek Greenbelt is a local treasure. On warm weekends when there's been sufficient rain, you'll see scores of people crowding around swimming holes and waterfalls to cool off. In cooler seasons, Austinites take to the trails in running shoes or with bags full of climbing gear.

A sunny, rocky trail leads down toward the creek.

The sculpted rocks by Sculpture Falls.

Along the trail, you'll spot an abundance of flora, including mustang grape, sideoats grama (Texas's state grass), even passionflower and Turk's cap. Snake-apple bears bright red fruits and American beautyberry bright purple balls that bloom in late summer. Dogwood and yaupon holly, live oak and American sycamore line the paths in a wash of green in early spring through late fall. You may even spot a bracted twistflower, a rare plant found only in Austin and Central Texas that grows on rocky slopes and produces pinkish blooms in April or May.

A rocky trail that runs alongside the creek.

As for wildlife, endangered golden-cheeked warblers nest in the area, and the Barton Springs and Austin blind salamander are rare amphibians that live nowhere else in the world except in and around Austin. You're unlikely to spot one, but the city is constantly working to protect them.

And along the whole trail flows Barton Creek, which travels 40 miles from Central Texas to Lady Bird Lake, part of the Edwards Aquifer and one of very few pristine streams in an urban area.

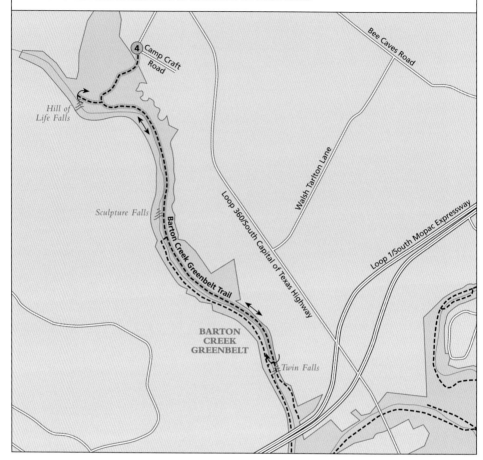

That said, the creek features vastly fluctuating water levels throughout the year depending on rainfall. During dry months, much of it is frequently little more than a puddle, but after an abundance of rainfall, the creek bed shimmers to life.

But to reach the creek, you'll have to descend the steep, rocky, cheekily named Hill of Life from the trailhead of the same name (sometimes also referred to as Trail's End as it is the terminus of Barton Creek Greenbelt trails). At 0.4 miles, veer right at a large, sunny clearing to head toward Hill of Life Falls where the trail flattens for most of the rest of the hike.

At 0.6 miles, a small dirt path will lead you straight down to the falls, which, during rainy seasons, are a pleasant place to take a dip among large limestone boulders.

From here, turn around and take the rocky dirt path to the right that follows alongside the creek. Several paths weave across the main trail from time to time, some of which lead down to the creek, but most return to the main trail in short order, so it's unlikely you'll get too far off course.

At 1.7 miles, take the short, narrow side trail to the right to Sculpture Falls. Here, limestone has been sculpted into soft curves by thousands of years of erosion, which makes for a unique geological landscape. During wetter months, water flows through and around the rock and over a falls a few feet high into a swimming hole below. During dryer months, there may not be any water to speak of, but the rock formations are still worth a look.

Head back up to the main path on any of the footpaths and continue heading down the trail with the creek on your right.

At about 3.0 miles, you will arrive at Twin Falls, which offers a picturesque place to stop, take a rest, have a picnic on the rocks, and take another dip. When you're ready, turn around and head back the way you came until 5.1 miles, when you will veer right two times before you run into the rocky hill you came down on the very first section of trail. Continue right up the wide, sunny, rocky trail to return to the trailhead.

MILES AND DIRECTIONS

0.0   Start from the Trail's End/Hill of Life Trailhead.

0.1   Veer right to continue down the wide, rocky path.

0.4   Turn right at the three-way intersection.

0.6   Arrive at Hill of Life Falls. Turn around and take the creekside trail to the right.

1.0   Continue straight at the junction with Barton Creek Greenbelt at mile marker 6.88.

1.7   Take the narrow path that veers off to the right to arrive at Sculpture Falls.

1.9   Keep right to continue on the Greenbelt Trail at mile marker 6.02.

3.0   Arrive at Twin Falls. Turn around to retrace your steps.

4.3   Arrive back at Sculpture Falls, veer right, then turn left at the mile marker a few steps ahead.

5.1   Veer right at the junction at marker 6.88.

5.2   Continue on the wide trail to the right at Barton Creek Greenbelt marker 6.99.

5.3   Turn right onto the wide, rocky trail from the start of the hike to return to the trailhead.

5.6   Veer left to continue on the wide rocky trail up the hill.

5.7   Arrive back at the trailhead.

5 MAYFIELD PARK AND PRESERVE LOOP: MAIN TRAIL, LAKE TRAIL, CREEK TRAIL

Shady woods, shallow creek crossings, river views, lush and vivid gardens populated by koi ponds and peacocks . . . this meandering stroll through a compact preserve is a refreshing urban oasis near downtown Austin. The hike itself may be short, but it's certainly sweet. So bring your camera, pose in front of the lilies, watch the peacocks strut and call from the gnarled branches of sprawling live oaks, and take it slow to truly appreciate your surroundings.

Start: Main Trail Trailhead
Elevation gain: 495 to 538 feet
Distance: 0.8-mile loop
Difficulty: Easy due to little elevation change, brevity, and plenty of shortcut opportunities
Hiking time: 20 minutes
Seasons/schedule: Open year-round 5 a.m.–10 p.m.
Fees and permits: None
Trail contacts: City of Austin Parks and Recreation Department, 200 S Lamar Blvd., Austin, TX 78704; (512) 974-6797; https://mayfieldpark.org
Canine compatibility: Dogs are not permitted anywhere in the park or gardens
Trail surface: Dirt, rock

Land status: Austin Parks and Recreation Department
Nearest town: Austin
Other trail users: Hikers only
Maps: Austin PARD, https://www .austintexas.gov/sites/default/files/ files/Parks/GIS/MayfieldKioskMap .pdf
Water availability: Yes
Special considerations: There is limited parking; if the lot is full, which happens often on weekends, holidays, and during the summer, there is on-street parking as well.
Amenities available: Port-a-potties available at the end of the parking lot
Maximum grade: 15% for 0.1 miles
Cell service: Throughout park

FINDING THE TRAILHEAD

From the parking lot, head to the right of the garden, which is surrounded by a low stone wall. A dirt path lined with stones will lead you down the trail.
GPS: 30.312800, -97.771617

Trail conditions: The trail is uneven and rocky in many places, a dirt path with roots and large rocks and several creek crossings. Most of it is in at least partial shade.

THE HIKE

As you approach Mayfield Park and Preserve, the first thing to likely catch your eye are the peacocks strutting along the low stone walls around the garden, flaunting their feathers high in the mature live oaks that provide dappled shade across the property. If you don't see them right away, you'll certainly hear them—a peacock call is far from melodious.

After you overcome the thrill of walking among such regal birds, the rest of the park and garden reveals itself: Colorful garden beds, reflecting ponds filled with koi,

Ferns, flowers, and native wildlife abound.

and greenery surround the historic Mayfield House. The quaint and picturesque board and batten cottage was originally a residence, but when Mary Mayfield Gutsch, who designed the lavish gardens during her tenure there, died in 1971, she left the home and acreage—plus an ostentation of peacocks—to the City of Austin to be used as a park.

The trail starts off to the right of the gardens. There will be a stone-lined dirt path leading to the start of the trail and a sign with a map of the trail system and a marker indicating where you are.

Peacocks roam freely on preserve grounds, mainly in the gardens.

As you begin, take your time as you identify Mexican persimmon trees, cedar elm, live oak, and Ashe juniper: The trail is brimming with Texas plants and many informative signs that identify various plants native to the area like Turks cap and silk tassel.

At the first signposted junction, turn left on the Meadow Loop trail, a short section that connects with the Taylor Creek Trail. This portion is lushly wooded and shady, but bring insect repellent in warmer months as several creeks make the area prime hunting grounds for mosquitos.

After crossing a creek via low stepping stones, turn left at the sign for the Taylor Creek Trail. Here, a narrower but smoother dirt path will lead you through woods filled with birdsong.

At the next four-way junction, there is a pleasant creek with a low stone bridge. Dip your feet in the water on a hot day, then veer right on either side of the creek—both ways loop around to the East Creek Trail and the difference in distance is hardly more than a few feet.

Continue right to stay on the Creek Trail loop. Taking any side trails to the left will take you back up to the garden, but entrance gates at those points are frequently locked.

You will cross another narrow, shallow creek and at the next four-way junction, turn right onto Taylor Creek Trail, but not before taking a quick detour up the dirt and reclaimed wooded staircase that curves up to the rocky cliffs on your left for a photo op.

In a few steps, you'll return to the beginning of the Taylor Creek Trail loop. Turn left to take the connector trail back to Meadow Loop, tiptoe back across the creek, up two sets of short dirt steps, and turn left onto Creek Trail.

At the next junction, Creek Trail turns into Lake Trail and a few steps later, a side trail will lead you down to a quiet, picturesque inlet off Lake Austin. It will only add a minute to your hike, but the views of the water and waterfront homes are well worth it.

A lake house across the creek on a waterfront portion of trail.

Expect a creek crossing or two on this short hike.

Afterward, continue up the rocky path past a sign for Creek Trail and turn left on Lakeview Trail. If, that is, you would indeed like to enjoy a lake view. At the lookout point complete with viewing deck, dwarf palmettos and live oaks covered with Spanish moss frame the view.

A fish pond within the preserve gardens.

When you've had your fill of lake views, head up the stone and wood steps behind you to return to the Lake Trail. At the top, turn left. You'll soon reach another marker that points straight ahead to Laguna Gloria, a modern gallery space, but turn right to head to the exit at the opposite end of the parking lot from where you started.

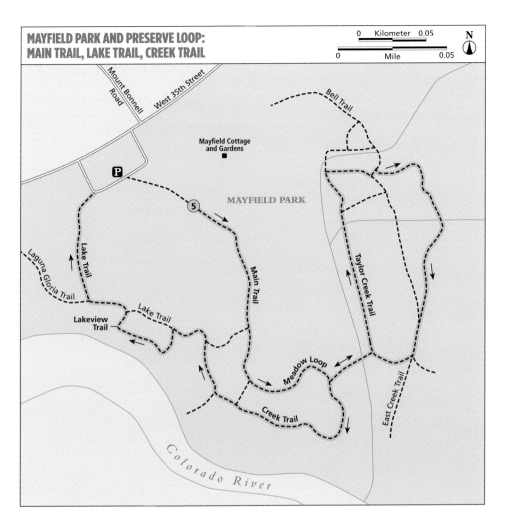

MILES AND DIRECTIONS

0.0 Start at the trailhead to the right of the garden.

0.1 The trail splits. Keep left to hike on Meadow Loop.

0.2 Turn left toward Taylor Creek Trail; cross the creek. Turn left to continue onto Taylor Creek Trail.

0.3 Turn right at the four-way trail junction at the creek with a low stone bridge. Turn right on East Creek Trail.

0.4 Turn left at the four-way junction onto Taylor Creek Trail. Turn left to take the connector trail back to Meadow Loop, across the creek, and up two sets of brief dirt steps.

0.5 Go left onto Creek Trail.

0.6 A side trail on the left leads to a view of Lake Austin/the Colorado River. Turn left at Lakeview Trail.

0.7 Arrive at Lookout Point. Turn left to return to Lake Trail.

0.8 Arrive back at the parking lot.

6 MOUNT BONNELL

This quick urban hike with sweeping views of downtown Austin and Texas Hill Country, plus stunning sunsets, is located just up the road from lovely Mayfield Preserve. You'll have to work for your views, but only briefly: The stairs leading to the top are guaranteed to get your heart pumping, but once you arrive at the top you'll see they were worth the effort.

Start: The staircase located on Mt. Bonnell Road
Elevation gain: 688 to 789 feet
Distance: 0.6-mile loop
Difficulty: Moderate due to steep steps
Hiking time: 20 minutes
Seasons/schedule: Year-round, open 5 a.m.–10 p.m.
Fees and permits: None
Trail contacts: Austin Parks and Recreation Department, 200 S Lamar Blvd., Austin, TX 78704; (512) 974-6797; https://www.austintexas .gov/page/historic-austin-parks
Canine compatibility: On-leash only
Trail surface: Dirt path with one constructed staircase
Land status: Austin Parks and Recreation
Nearest town: Austin
Other trail users: Hikers only

Maps: USGS Austin West Quadrangle, https://maps.lib.utexas .edu/maps/topo/texas/geopdf_2013/ austin_west-2013.pdf, http://www .austinexplorer.com/Locations/Show Location.aspx?LocationID=1791
Water availability: None
Special considerations: Parking fills up fast on summer afternoons and on weekends. If there's no street parking available, consider parking down the road as far as Mayfield Park and Preserve and walking to the trailhead. Most of this trail is in full sun, so wear protective clothing and bring sunscreen and plenty of water.
Amenities available: Limited picnic tables near the summit and at the bottom of the hill; no bathrooms
Maximum grade: 25% for 0.1 miles
Cell service: Available throughout

FINDING THE TRAILHEAD

On Mt. Bonnell Road, look for the wide stone steps behind the rows of parked cars. **GPS:** 30.321414, -97.772943

Trail conditions: Most of the trail is solid packed dirt, wide and accommodating, though the first section of the hike is a constructed stone staircase. Short side trails are steep and rocky, and on the hike down there are often large chunks of limestone to step down or around.

THE HIKE

Mount Bonnell, located within Covert Park on Austin's hilly west side, offers some of the best views in the city, and locals know it. It is often packed on weekends, but evenings and weekdays are lovely times to visit as crowds thin, leaving more space to enjoy expansive views of Austin's skyline to the east and Hill Country to the south and west. Make the trek up the 102 stairs near sunset for a natural show as the sun dips behind the tree-covered hills across the Colorado River.

It's been a popular tourist destination since the 1850s, but the park and summit were officially given to the people of the city in 1939 by F. M. Covert Sr. and his family, who

A view of the Colorado River, also known as Lake Austin, from near the top of Mount Bonnell.

owned the land. Today, it's still cited as one of the most romantic spots in Austin, prompting plenty of picnics and proposals.

Start your hike by taking the stairs up from the road and the parking area. There is a handrail to assist you. When you reach the top, take a few minutes to catch your breath and enjoy the views from the stone viewing deck and pavilion as you watch the sun sparkle off the Lake Austin portion of the Colorado River below and boats cruise the blue waters.

Top left: Stone steps lead down to small overlooks.
Top right: The river snakes toward downtown Austin and beyond.
Bottom: Downtown Austin in the distance.

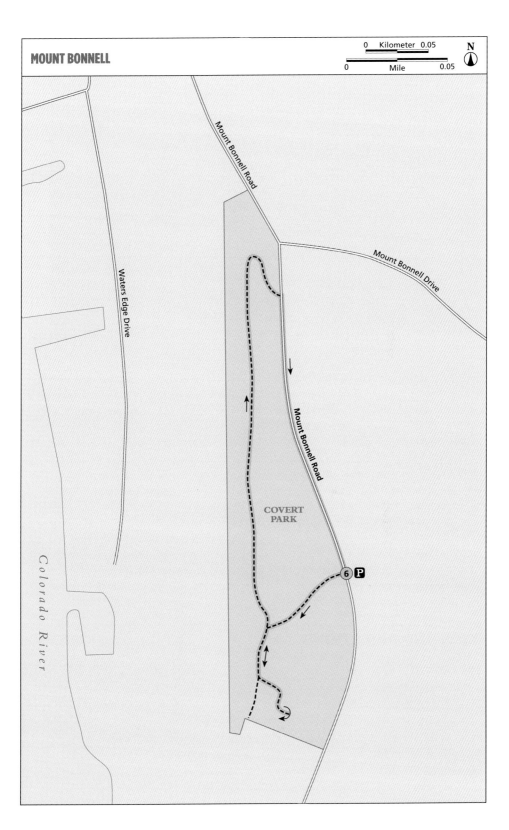

0   Kilometer   0.05

N

0   Mile   0.05

Mount Bonnell Road

Mount Bonnell Drive

Waters Edge Drive

Mount Bonnell Road

COVERT
PARK

6 P

Colorado River

The Colorado River far below.

Meander down the trail to your left to find views of the ever-evolving city of Austin skyline, then, if you're feeling exploratory, climb down one or two of the steep, rocky trails from this lookout to find small pockets of seclusion. The side trails don't go far, so don't worry about getting lost.

After enjoying the views from the summit, continue to the right down the wide dirt path as you head downhill. There are plenty more lookouts along the way, some even better than at the summit, so don't put your camera away yet! You'll be able to see far down the stretch of Lake Austin, plus plenty of rolling Hill Country landscape covered in greenery and peppered with multimillion-dollar homes.

On the non–cliff side of the trail, live oak, Texas kidneywood, Ashe juniper, and even red yucca, which sprouts bright pink blooms in the spring, grow alongside the trail and out of the limestone walls, as do a smattering of wildflowers in the spring.

Once you reach the end of the developed trail, take care as you walk back to your car, as you will be doing so on the edge of the road. Cars generally drive slowly here but proceed with caution.

MILES AND DIRECTIONS

- **0.0** Start at the base of the staircase.
- **0.1** Reach the viewing deck at the top of the stairs, and head left for better views of the downtown city skyline and a few very short dead-end trails; turn around.
- **0.2** Lookouts begin and continue down the remainder of trail.
- **0.4** Reach the end of the trail, and take a sharp right turn to head back toward the road and parking area.
- **0.6** Arrive back at the stairs at the beginning of the trail.

7 WILD BASIN WILDERNESS PRESERVE PARK LOOP

This short hike close to Austin offers a surprisingly quiet and picturesque escape into nature. While you may hear road sounds from nearby Loop 360 at a few points along the trail, more often, dense forest and chattering creeks and waterfalls invite you to imagine you're a world away from civilization. Bonus: The St. Edwards University Wild Basin Creative Research Center is located at the trailhead and offers educational opportunities to visitors and plenty of educational signage.

Start: Arroyo Vista Loop Trailhead
Elevation gain: 679 to 901 feet
Distance: 1.8-mile loop
Difficulty: Easy due to length but with some elevation gain and rocky trails
Hiking time: 1 hour
Seasons/schedule: Year-round, open sunrise to sunset
Fees and permits: Free on weekdays, $5 on weekends and holidays when reservations are required when visiting from 7:30 a.m.–5:30 p.m.
Trail contacts: St. Edwards University, 805 N. Capital of Texas Hwy., Austin, TX, 78746; (512) 327-7622; https://www.stedwards.edu/wild-basin/visit
Canine compatibility: No dogs allowed

Trail surface: Dirt, rock
Land status: Co-owned and co-managed by Travis County and St. Edward's University
Nearest town: Austin
Other trail users: Hikers only
Maps: St. Edwards University, https://stedwards.app.box.com/s/zadugppyn4yob432dio9ms90jnqti74z
Water availability: None when research center is closed
Special considerations: Parking is limited, and the entrance gate will close when the parking area is full.
Amenities available: Restrooms at the trailhead, information center with shaded porch
Maximum grade: 13% for 0.2 miles
Cell service: Throughout

FINDING THE TRAILHEAD

From Loop 360 or North Capital of Texas Highway, turn onto the park road (there will be a sign at the entrance). Drive down the road to the parking area. The trailhead will be on the far end of the lot nearest the research center. An information sign features a scannable QR code that links to a map and trail info is posted. **GPS:** 30.310506, -97.823790

Trail conditions: The trail begins as packed dirt sprinkled with gravel. Arroyo Vista Loop is stroller-friendly. But then the trail becomes rocky and uneven with sections of large step-downs and several creek crossings. Much of the trail is in at least partial shade.

THE HIKE

Rolling green hills, white and gray limestone, trickling creeks, and shaggy juniper await at this unique property just minutes from downtown Austin. Here, you'll find nearly 3 miles of trails, mostly shaded paths with a bit of elevation change, and a designated Important Bird Area, partially due to the presence of the endangered golden–cheeked warbler.

A wooden footbridge spans a divide.

But also located within this picturesque 227-acre preserve is the St. Edwards University Wild Basin Creative Research Center, which not only serves as a living laboratory for university students and faculty, but also houses a visitor gallery that hosts environmental education programs for students of all ages and where hikers and students can learn about and interact with nature.

The hiking trails begin at the end of the parking lot. So from the informational sign by the parking lot, veer left on Arroyo Vista Loop, keeping the center on your right. Almost

Greenery surrounds this quiet trail.

immediately, the trail will split; head to the left for a brief detour to a scenic viewpoint or continue straight to stay on the main trail as you pass the center.

Then, enjoy the views. Yaupon holly, oaks, juniper, and yucca line the path that's often wide enough for two and fairly flat. Shortly, the trees will open up to expansive views of hillsides covered with juniper and peppered with homes nestled in the dense foliage.

Golden afternoon light along the trail.

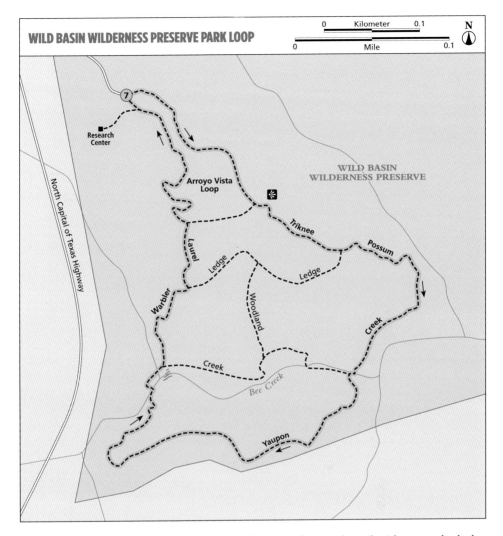

0   Kilometer   0.1

0   Mile   0.1

N

WILD BASIN
WILDERNESS PRESERVE

Research
Center

Arroyo Vista
Loop

Triknee

Possum

Laurel

Ledge

Warbler

Ledge

Woodland

Creek

Creek

Bee Creek

North Capital of Texas Highway

Yaupon

At 0.3 miles, continue onto Triknee Trail and find a side trail with an overlook that reconnects just up the trail. Here, a winding gravel and rock path will lead you downhill over the next half-mile or so.

After descending some steps, continue straight onto Possum Trail and watch your feet as you continue to hike down over uneven, rocky terrain with a few large step-downs. There is more shade on this portion of trail thanks to mature juniper and Buckley's oak.

When you reach the creek at 0.7 miles, sit and enjoy the view before you cross and continue on. As soon as you do, turn left onto Yaupon Trail and start heading back uphill on a rocky, uneven path with some steps but also a few welcome flat sections.

At 1.3 miles, arrive at a creek and small waterfall. In dryer months, there won't be much of a cascade to speak of, but the limestone creek bed and fern-covered banks make it a pleasant, shady place to sit and have a snack or enjoy the scenery. The habitat is fragile, so hikers are asked to stay out of the water.

A stairway into a juniper forest.

As you continue, turn left onto Warbler Trail, following signs for the trailhead. You'll continue to ascend as you work your way back up in elevation after descending to the creek.

At 1.5 miles, turn left to take Laurel Trail. When you run back into Arroyo Vista Loop, turn left again to continue to the trailhead and in no time you'll pass a manmade chimney swift tower that offers these special birds a place to nest and be back at the research center.

MILES AND DIRECTIONS

- **0.0** Start from the Arroyo Vista Loop Trailhead.
- **0.1** Continue straight at the junction with a connector trail on your right.
- **0.3** At the junction with Arroyo Vista Loop and Triknee Trail, take the connecting lookout point trail to your left.
- **0.4** At the intersection with Ledge and Possum Trails, continue straight onto Possum.
- **0.7** Cross the creek then turn left onto Yaupon Trail at the junction with Creek and Yaupon Trails.
- **1.3** Arrive at the creek and a small waterfall. Continue straight across. At the junction with Creek, Yaupon, and Warbler, turn left onto Warbler following the signs for the trailhead.
- **1.5** Turn left onto Laurel Trail at the intersection with Ledge, Warbler, and Laurel Trails.
- **1.6** Turn left on Arroyo Vista Loop to continue to the trailhead.
- **1.8** Pass the connector trail to the other side of Arroyo Vista Loop, a chimney swift tower, and the Wild Basin Creative Research Center.
- **1.8** Arrive back at the trailhead.

8 EMMA LONG METRO PARK TURKEY CREEK TRAIL

This lovely, shaded trail located within Austin's city limits is a favorite among dog owners; four-legged hikers are allowed to run free over the nearly 3 miles of creeks and trails. But two-legged visitors will also enjoy the quiet, shaded paths, trickling creeks, and occasional vistas.

Start: Turkey Creek Trail parking lot and trailhead
Elevation gain: 518 to 665 feet
Distance: 2.9-mile lollipop
Difficulty: Easy to moderate due to numerous creek crossings and one steep section
Hiking time: 1 hour, 30 minutes
Seasons/schedule: Year-round, open 7 a.m.–10 p.m.
Fees and permits: Free but to enter the park proper down the road, which features a campground, swimming area, and boat ramp, is $5 per vehicle per day Mon–Thurs and $10 Fri–Sun
Trail contacts: Austin Parks and Recreation Department, 200 S. Lamar Blvd., Austin, TX 78704; (512) 974-6700; https://www.austintexas .gov/department/emma-long -metropolitan-park
Canine compatibility: Off-leash dogs permitted
Trail surface: Dirt
Land status: Austin Parks and Recreation
Nearest town: Austin
Other trail users: Hikers only
Maps: Austin Parks Department, https://www.austintexas.gov/sites/ default/files/files/Parks/GIS/Emma LongKioskMap_TurkeyCk.pdf
Water availability: No
Special considerations: The park can get very busy on weekends.
Amenities available: Porta potty, picnic tables
Maximum grade: 25% for 0.1 miles
Cell service: Cell service throughout

FINDING THE TRAILHEAD

From City Park Road, drive past the sign for Emma Long Metropark, continue 2 miles, and find the trailhead parking lot on the right.
GPS: 30.333505, -97.839995
Trail conditions: The trail is packed dirt and frequently peppered with rocks, roots, and stones, but it is wide and accommodating. After prolonged or heavy rain, more than half a dozen creek crossings mean you'll likely get your feet wet. Most of the trail is pleasantly shaded.

THE HIKE

Dog lovers rejoice! On this peaceful, shady trail within a city park, four-legged hiking companions can frolic leash-free down the wide paths and at plenty of creek crossings. The trail is a favorite among pet owners, especially on weekends, so arrive early to score a parking spot or visit on weekdays when you'll enjoy a bit more solitude. Then hit the trail for a well-marked hike through Ashe juniper forest.

The trail itself starts out rocky and uneven, but variation defines the route: it's wide and then narrow, rocky then smooth, flat then steep, lined with mature live oaks then yaupon holly and Ashe juniper, which the endangered golden-cheeked warbler nests in in the spring. The only constant: the ever-present creek.

The uneven and rocky trail is often lined with juniper.

While the creek is shallow to nonexistent in drier months and you can ford most crossings without getting your feet wet, in wetter seasons, you may want to bring hiking sandals or an extra pair of socks. But despite frequent zigzagging across the water, the trail is well maintained and marked: Wooden trail signs with white arrows direct you.

You'll begin and end on the same section of trail, but at the three-quarter-mile mark, the loop begins, and while you can proceed in either direction, we suggest you veer left

Expect several creek crossings throughout the hike.

across the creek to tackle the loop clockwise. This will lead you to a small waterfall and pool at the 0.9-mile mark, which is a picturesque spot to sit and listen or watch dogs play as you search for crayfish under and around the rocks and listen to the soft trickle of water and the melodious birdsong emanating from the woods.

At 1.0 mile, the woods become more verdant. Ashe junipers still dominate the landscape, but more green foliage sprouts low to the ground, coloring the landscape. At

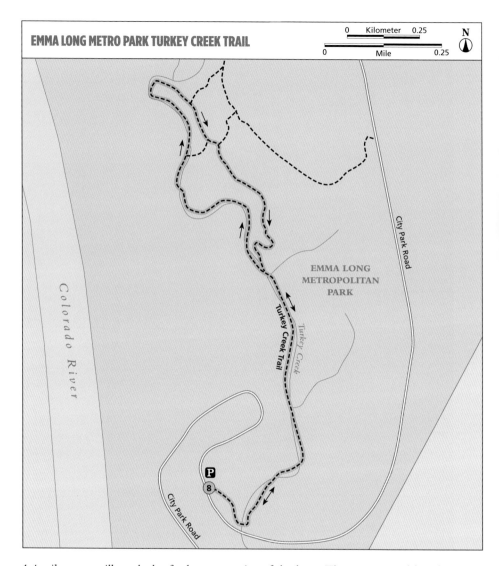

0   Kilometer   0.25   N

0   Mile   0.25

Colorado River

City Park Road

EMMA LONG
METROPOLITAN
PARK

Turkey Creek Trail

Turkey Creek

City Park Road

P

8

1.4 miles, you will reach the furthermost point of the loop. There are several benches if you'd like to sit and rest and enjoy the scenery before the rocky trail starts to ascend. Here, you can catch a glimpse of the surrounding landscape between branches as you crest the hill where the trail opens up, if only for a few minutes, as tall, dense juniper give way to short, green bushes.

For a moment, instead of woods flanking the trail, enjoy the sun on your face and a variety of grasses, plus the occasional yucca and prickly pear cactus. At 1.7 miles, the trail starts to descend almost as quickly as it ascended and as you hike down the rocky path, you'll return to shadier sections of trail.

At 2.0 miles, you will complete the lollipop loop and be back on the trail you started on. Retrace your steps from the first 0.7 miles to return to the trailhead.

Left: Native plants line the shady trail.
Right: Most creek crossings feature stepping stones, but be prepared to get your feet wet after heavy rains.

MILES AND DIRECTIONS

0.0 Start at the trailhead signage in the corner of the parking lot.

0.1 Arrive at your first creek crossing.

0.7 The lollipop loop begins; take the trail to the left.

1.4 Find benches on which to rest before the trail ascends.

2.0 Complete the loop and return to the out-and-back portion of the trail. Retrace your steps to the parking lot.

2.9 Arrive back at the trailhead and parking lot.

9 RIVER PLACE NATURE TRAIL

This 5.5-mile trail isn't for the faint of heart: with 2,836 built-in steps and 1,700 feet of elevation gain each way, it's one of the most challenging hikes in Hill Country. That makes it a popular trail for training if you have bigger, more ambitious hikes in mind outside of Hill Country, but it is also a pleasant and enjoyable, if strenuous, hike not far from downtown Austin.

Start: The Panther Hollow Trail Trailhead on Big View Drive
Elevation gain: 501 to 893 feet
Distance: 5.6-mile out-and-back
Difficulty: Difficult due to steep grades and lots of steps
Hiking time: 3 hours
Seasons/schedule: Open year-round, sunrise to sunset
Fees and permits: None on weekdays, $10 fee per hiker on Sat, Sun, and holidays
Trail contacts: River Place LD, 14050 Summit Dr., Suite 103, Austin, TX 78728; (512) 246-0498; http://www.riverplacelimiteddistrict.org/trails.html
Canine compatibility: On-leash only
Trail surface: Dirt
Land status: Neighborhood park

Nearest town: Austin
Other trail users: Hikers only
Maps: River Place Limited District, http://www.riverplacelimiteddistrict.org/trails.html, https://nebula.wsimg.com/1c776977fd86c47e8739aec89f95baef?AccessKeyId=5F4DA48D31454086C5DC&disposition=0&alloworigin=1
Water availability: Located at Woodlands Park down the road
Special considerations: On-street parking only.
Amenities available: Restrooms, picnic tables, and playground at Woodlands Park down the road
Maximum grade: 30% for 0.3 miles
Cell service: Throughout, though may be spotty in places

FINDING THE TRAILHEAD

On Big View Drive, look for the pond with fountain and boardwalk. The trailhead begins at the sidewalk. **GPS:** 30.35785154861606, -97.86413157308733
Trail conditions: The trail is well-packed dirt but often rocky with lots of steep sections that feature built-in stair steps. It's typically only wide enough for one or two and is only partially shaded.

THE HIKE

River Place Nature Trail offers a little bit of everything: sections of smooth dirt paths, rocky surfaces, waterfalls and creeks, stairs, shade, sun, and aggressive inclines and declines. It is a popular trail among trail runners and you will occasionally see Austin-area hikers blazing the paths with heavy packs to prepare for more aggressive and difficult trails farther afield.

But you'll also see groups of friends and families out for an afternoon stroll, with or without the family pet in tow, as it offers several sections of less-aggressive terrain and pleasantly cool creeks for mid-hike cooldowns.

You can start at either the Panther Hollow Trailhead or Canyon Trail Trailhead, but we recommend Panther Hollow to put the most challenging section of trail in the middle of the hike instead of the beginning and the end. So start at the boardwalk beside

One of many rustic staircases along the trail.

the pond, complete with fountain, where there is a map, information about the trail, trash cans, and a couple of picnic tables. There are a few rocking chairs and a bench along the boardwalk so you can sit and enjoy the view before or after your hike, but at 0.1 miles, veer left to take the dirt path away from the pond. Here, the stair steps begin.

As do thick growths of Ashe juniper, cedar elm, and sugarberry that line the trail alongside a plethora of vines, native grasses, and false dayflower with tiny purple blooms

A small waterfall offers a place to rest and cool off in the summer.

that can be found in the spring. Twisting arms of live oak trees bend over the creek and the trail, providing welcome shade, and limestone cliffs flank the trail on your left as the shallow, chattering creek flows on your right.

In half a mile, you'll pass the junction with Little Fern Trail. Continue straight on Canyon Trail. There are metal signs posted on trees along the way at frequent intervals informing you of the distance to either trailhead. They also feature emergency codes in case you have to call for help and need to identify your location.

A mature Ashe juniper along the trail.

At 0.9 miles, take a break at the small swimming hole, complete with dwarf waterfall, a pleasant place to sit and relax, have a snack, rehydrate, dip your toes, or let the dogs play. Another such picturesque spot awaits just down the trail. Take your time, because after this point, instead of sporadic and brief ups and downs, the trail starts ascending in earnest.

At 1.5 miles, and again at 1.8, you'll cross a creek. There are stones to help keep your feet out of the water, and also a chain to hold onto to help you keep your balance. This

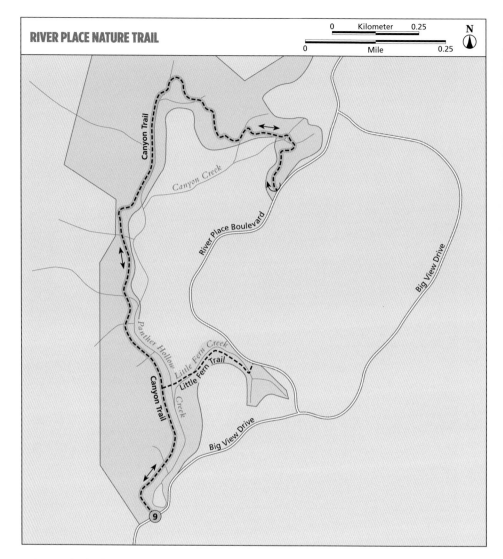

point marks the beginning of the most strenuous section of trail, a mile of almost endless ascent, mostly made of stairs.

While most of the trail up to this point is in partial, dappled shade unique to the sparsely leafed live oak and juniper of Hill Country, foliage begins to thin a bit and in spots where the trail opens up and there is less tree cover, look for prickly pear cactus.

At 1.9 miles and again at 2.1, continue straight through what looks like a trail junction (the intersecting paths dead-end onto private property). Shortly after, you'll enter something of a clearing with a bench and be able to take a break at the end of the long climb and enjoy unobstructed views of the surrounding tree-covered hills.

At 2.8 miles, after a bit more uphill climb, you will reach the Canyon Trail Trailhead. There is another map here, along with a pair of benches and some shade so you can sit, rest, and have a snack before you turn around and retrace your steps back to Panther Hollow.

The boardwalk and pond at the start and end of the trail.

MILES AND DIRECTIONS

0.0   Start at the Panther Hollow Trail Trailhead at the beginning of the boardwalk next to the pond.

0.1   The trail turns to the left on a dirt path with steps.

0.5   Continue straight onto Canyon Trail at the junction with Little Fern Trail.

1.5   Cross the creek.

1.8   Cross another creek. Do so again just around the bend.

1.9   Continue straight through the junction.

2.1   At the junction, continue straight up the steps.

2.2   Reach the top of the hill and a small clearing with a bench and a view.

2.8   Arrive at Canyon Trail Trailhead. Turn around and retrace your steps.

5.6   Arrive back at Panther Hollow Trail Trailhead.

> Hikers frequently underestimate the difficulty of this trail and/or do not bring adequate water or food, so make sure you come prepared.

10 GREENWAY PRIMITIVE TRAIL AT BEE CAVE

This suburban oasis may be more popular with neighborhood residents than it is with visitors, but it offers a fantastic option for a fairly leisurely stroll in nature. It's especially popular among trail runners for its wide, sunny paths and fairly level terrain and is even peppered with trash cans and benches for hikers more interested in taking their time than checking off miles. Along the way, you can expect scenic views, plenty of native plants, and even spot area wildlife.

Start: The Greenway Primitive Trailhead begins at the far end of the small trailhead parking lot
Elevation gain: 966 to 1,177 feet
Distance: 3.4-mile lollipop
Difficulty: Easy due to little elevation change but can be more difficult in summer due to sparse shade for most of the route
Hiking time: 1.5 hours
Seasons/schedule: Year-round
Fees and permits: None
Trail contacts: City of Bee Cave Parks and Recreation, 4000 Galleria Parkway, Bee Cave, TX 78738; (512) 767-6617; https://www.beecavetexas.gov/city-government/departments/parks-recreation/trails

Canine compatibility: Dogs allowed
Trail surface: Dirt
Land status: City of Bee Cave park
Nearest town: Bee Cave
Other trail users: Mountain bikes
Maps: City of Bee Cave, https://www.beecavetexas.gov/home/showpublisheddocument/1041/635284252021870000
Water availability: None
Special considerations: The trail is located in a neighborhood, so be mindful of speed, volume, and where you park. Bring plenty of water with you as there's none nearby.
Amenities available: None
Maximum grade: 25% for 0.25 miles
Cell service: Yes, throughout

FINDING THE TRAILHEAD

From TX 71, turn north onto Vail Divide into the Canyonside at Falconhead West neighborhood, then take an immediate left onto Rockies Run Summit and another immediate left onto Patagonia Pass. The trailhead parking lot will be immediately on your right. **GPS:** 30.31946, -97.99567

Trail conditions: The trail consists of sections of packed dirt, crushed gravel, and uneven rock. Most of it is in full sun.

THE HIKE

What this area lacks in directional signage it makes up for in sparsely populated trails and an abundance of hiking options thanks to a number of looping trails that interconnect, offering hikers the option to customize their route if they prefer a quicker jaunt over the hills and through the woods or the full loop. But no matter which route you take, prepare to wend your way through fragrant juniper, abundant yucca, even patches of wildflowers in the spring.

The mostly sunny trail starts off in a small parking lot and for the first few minutes meanders behind the fenced backyards of impressive neighborhood homes. In fact, you'll see plenty of Hill Country residences as you hike the various loops. When the thick

Trails are occasionally rocky and narrow.

Top: Sunny trails on grassy hillsides.
Bottom left: The sign by the trailhead parking lot.
Bottom right: Wildflowers punctuate the trail in the spring and summer.

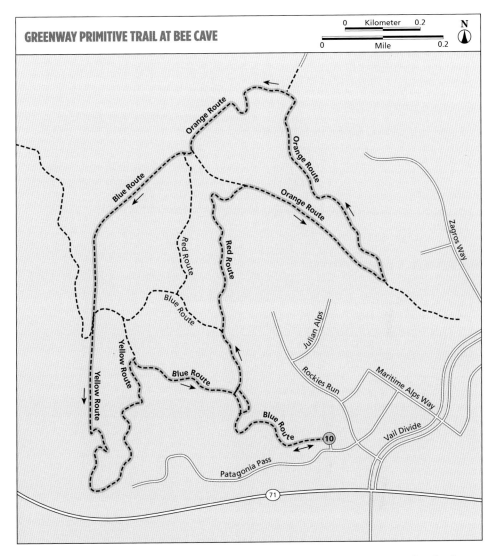

stands of Ashe juniper that line the trails give way to views of the surrounding landscape, that is.

Start on the Blue Route, where you can expect some shade in the morning and evening but bright sun overhead throughout most of the afternoon. In fact, any shaded sections offer partial shade at most, so come prepared in warmer months with a hat, sunscreen, and plenty of water. At the first metal trail marker, continue onto the Red Route, where you'll experience a fairly steep downhill section before turning right onto the Orange Route.

Intermittent steep sections of trail will continue, but most are over almost as soon as they begin. At the junction where the Orange Route splits, follow the sign pointing left toward the Greenway Primitive Trail, not toward the City of Bee Cave path, which will take you back to the neighborhood. As soon as you turn left, bear left again. The trail looks like it veers to the right, but that trail also takes you back toward the neighborhood.

At the next junction that looks like an intersection of four trails, continue straight onto the Red Route. A few steps later, at the next intersection, turn right onto the Blue Route.

Continue on the Blue Route until you reach the junction with the Yellow Route, then continue straight on the trail that stretches between an apartment complex on your right and dense foliage on your left.

Finally, at the stone marker that signals the intersection of the Yellow and Blue Route, turn right to head back toward the trailhead.

Take note that while many narrow side trails exist, they often connect back to the main trail. Intersections aren't always well marked, so it's a good idea to bring either a printed or digital map and track your progress so you don't get lost. Fortunately, there are frequent trail locator signs that also serve as markers. Each features a number and instructions to call 911 if you get lost or injured so that you can give your precise location to emergency services.

MILES AND DIRECTIONS

0.0 Start at the Greenway Primitive Trail Trailhead parking lot.

0.2 Turn right onto Blue Route.

0.3 Continue straight on Red Route.

0.6 Turn right onto Orange Route.

1.4 Continue onto Red Route, then in a few steps, turn right onto Blue Route.

2.0 Continue straight onto Yellow Route.

2.5 Turn right at the junction with Blue Route and retrace your steps from the first 0.2 miles.

3.4 Arrive back at the trailhead.

11 LAKEWAY CANYONLANDS TRAIL

On this hike, the journey is more rewarding than the destination: Finding a route is half the fun on this winding trail system beloved by hikers and mountain bikers alike—those who know about it, anyway. As is the challenge of navigating the wooded trails and switchbacks that lead you to the summit. The hike involves plenty of ascending, followed by plenty of descending, but mostly shaded woods and sun-speckled rocky trails make for an exceedingly pleasant challenge, one of the longest inclines in the area, in fact. As a bonus, even though the trailhead is located in a neighborhood, you're unlikely to cross paths with more than a handful of other outdoorists.

Start: Canyonlands Trailhead
Elevation gain: 797 to 1,179 feet
Distance: 4.7-mile out-and-back
Difficulty: Moderate to difficult due to prolonged climbs and rocky terrain
Hiking time: About 2.5 hours
Seasons/schedule: Year-round
Fees and permits: None
Trail contacts: City of Lakeway, 1102 Lohmans Crossing Rd., Lakeway, TX 78734; (512) 314-7500; https://www.lakeway-tx.gov/131/Canyonlands
Canine compatibility: On-leash only
Trail surface: Dirt, gravel
Land status: City of Lakeway
Nearest town: Lakeway
Other trail users: Mountain bikers
Maps: City of Lakeway, https://www.lakeway-tx.gov/DocumentCenter/View/431/Map---Canyonlands-Trail-2020-PDF?bidId= , https://www.lakeway-tx.gov/DocumentCenter/View/17030/Canyonlands-Map-2-JPG?bidId=
Water availability: Located at the bathroom building 0.4 miles into the hike
Special considerations: There's no water at the trailhead, but there is water 0.4 miles into the hike.
Amenities available: Bathroom, bike repair station, water fountains and a bottle-filling station, picnic tables are located a 0.4-mile hike from the trailhead
Maximum grade: 26% for 0.75 miles
Cell service: Available throughout

FINDING THE TRAILHEAD

From Lakeway Boulevard, turn south onto Highlands Boulevard and take an immediate left onto Trophy Drive. Trailhead parking is available along Trophy Drive and at Swim Center Park at 3103 Lakeway Blvd.
GPS: 30.34981, -97.99666
Trail conditions: Most sections of the trail are narrow and rocky with plenty of roots, but the trail is partially shaded and pleasant, even in summer. There are several fairly steep sections and a prolonged ascent.

THE HIKE

Canyonlands Park in the midst of the Lakeway neighborhood is the result of a gift to the city from the Lakeway Municipal Utilities District, and what a gift it is with winding, picturesque, varied, and often shaded trails built by local volunteer organization Friends of the Parks. The whole area provides a challenge to hikers, both navigationally and

Top: Several sunny sections run alongside power lines.
Bottom: Wildflowers bloom in the spring and early summer.

A painted wooden sign marks one possible way up to the summit.

physically, as most of the tree-lined paths are well maintained but not always terribly well marked, making a digital map helpful to keep fear of getting lost at bay.

Fortunately, a myriad of side trails loop back around and intersect, offering a chance for a bit of variety on your way up and back down. Several trail signs along the path include QR codes with a link to a rough map of the area. These QR codes, together with emergency locator markers, offer some direction and peace of mind.

The entrance to the Canyonlands trail system is accessible via a 0.25-mile gravel and dirt access trail that passes through city and Lakeway Municipal Utilities District property. To start, head toward the rock-lined path near the water tank that is marked with a sign that says "Canyonlands Trail built by Friends of the Park."

At the very first junction, turn left. For the next quarter mile, you can either follow the wide gravel trail next to the power lines or take the more pleasant and mostly shaded winding route that curves in and out of juniper forest. When you pass what looks like a maintenance building, curve to the right, then, on your left, across the maintenance path, a purple marker will guide you to the trail.

In a few steps you'll reach the first major junction complete with a well-stocked bathroom, bike repair station, and water fountain. From there, follow signs for the High Trail, then, at the junction with a picnic table, take the Canyon Trail. You'll start heading down in short order. The trail gets steep here and large rocks and roots pepper the trail, so take your time.

Continue on the Canyon Trail past two more intersections and a sturdy footbridge. Follow signs for Canyon and Lakeway trails as you begin to make your way out of the canyon. When you reach the junction with Mount Lakeway Trail, get ready for narrow and rugged but fairly well-maintained paths and to start heading uphill.

Left: Painted wooden signs mark several optional winding routes.
Right: A steep, sunny route offers a more direct alternative but less picturesque.

From here, much of the way is in partial shade, but bring sunscreen as there are plenty of exposed sections, though they are brief. The abundant juniper and live oak don't offer complete cover but enough to give some relief from the summer sun. When you reach a clearing full of grasses and wildflowers in the spring in the shadow of power lines, cross diagonally to the right to where the trail picks up again in the tree line on the other side at rescue marker 37.

Shortly after, cross a maintenance road to the path marked "Camelback." For much of the rest of the hike up, several narrow trails intersect but all lead to the peak. It is easy to feel like you are lost, but as long as you stay on a trail, you will eventually get to the top.

When you reach a second sunny junction, continue straight across the wide maintenance path toward the sign for "Dropout." Past the next maintenance road with a large metal gate, follow the Mount Lakeway trail marker to the left and continue on the curving switchbacks up the hill, often popping out into the sun near the wide path flanked by power lines and then swerving right back into the woods where the trail is more shaded and pleasant (but by no means direct).

As you near the summit, enjoy views of the surrounding hills, yucca, Texas madrone trees, occasional flourishes of wildflowers, live oaks, and plenty of juniper.

At the summit, a brand-new housing development doesn't offer much in the way of views, but you can still enjoy vistas of natural scenery, including of Lake Travis in the distance.

When it's time to start heading back down, simply retrace your steps. You can also take the sunnier, steeper, more rugged gravel and stone path that follows the power lines a

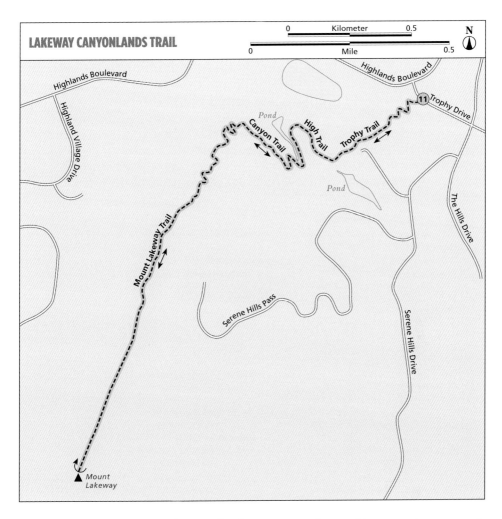

good chunk of the way if you prefer. If you want to take on a bit more, when you reach the start of Lakeway Trail, take the Canyon Trail or Pond Trail loop to extend your hike around these humble ponds.

MILES AND DIRECTIONS

0.0 Start at the Canyonlands Trailhead on Trophy Drive.

0.3 Turn right at High Trail.

0.4 Pass the restrooms, water fountain, and bike repair station.

0.5 Continue onto Canyon Trail.

0.6   Cross the footbridge.

0.9 Turn left on Lakeway Trail.

2.6 Reach the top of Mount Lakeway; turn around to retrace your steps.

4.7 Arrive back at the trailhead.

12 MILTON REIMERS RANCH RIVER LOOP

Once privately owned property, this park is popular with hikers, bikers, climbers, and Texas native plant enthusiasts. And this hike in particular lets you experience many of the ecosystems and landscapes that the park has to offer, from dry savannahs to riparian valleys to refreshing riverbeds. The upper portion of the trail is even accessible to bikes. Altogether, it offers a pleasant place to stroll with friends and take a dip in the inviting Pedernales River.

Start: Climbers Canyon Trailhead
Elevation gain: 683 to 808 feet
Distance: 4.0-mile loop
Difficulty: Easy to moderate due to mostly flat trail with several sections of steep inclines and full sun
Hiking time: 2 hours
Seasons/schedule: Park open daily, 7 a.m. to civil twilight
Fees and permits: Day-use fee 3+ $5, $3 for seniors, children 12 and under free. Cash only.
Trail contacts: Travis Country Parks, 23610 Hamilton Rd., Dripping Springs, TX 78620; (512) 264-1923; https://parks.traviscountytx.gov/parks/reimers-ranch
Canine compatibility: On-leash only

Trail surface: Dirt, rock, crushed granite
Land status: Travis Country Parks
Nearest town: Dripping Springs, Bee Cave
Other trail users: Bikes on second half of trail
Maps: Travis County Parks, https://parks.traviscountytx.gov/files/docs/reimers-map.pdf
Water availability: Yes
Special considerations: This trail is largely in full sun, so bring plenty of water and sun protection.
Amenities available: Restrooms, picnic tables, shelter
Maximum grade: 10% for 0.3 miles
Cell service: Spotty throughout

FINDING THE TRAILHEAD

 From Hilton Pool Road, turn onto Milton Reimers Ranch Road by the park entrance sign. Continue down the road for 3.1 miles to the parking area at Reimers Pavilion. The Climbers Canyon Trailhead is behind and to the left of the single drop-toilet bathroom at the southeast end of the parking lot.
GPS: 30.363645, -98.123418

Trail conditions: Most of the trail is in full sun as it transitions between rocky landscape to narrow dirt track to wide crushed gravel paths. Part of it follows along the riverbank.

THE HIKE

In 2005, Milton Reimers, the park's namesake, sold 2,427 acres of his land to Travis County to be used as a public park and to preserve lands. Now, the largest park in the county is a haven for mountain bikers, rock climbers, and hikers and boasts an abundance of primitive and groomed trails for all to enjoy.

Reimer's Ranch charges an entry fee and does not accept credit cards. Bring cash or you will be denied entry. Reservations are not required except for observatory programs in the Dark Sky Park.

The Pedernales River flowing next to the trail.

Among them, the Upper and Lower River Trail that follows alongside the Pedernales River and the Hike and Bike Trail, a flatter and more accessible path flanked by native plants, wildlife, and views of the valley below.

And while the first half of the trail tends to be narrow and uneven in spots with brief rolling ups and downs, the second half offers easy strolling in the sun. Along the former, there are ample opportunities for swimming or lounging by the river, and on the latter, informational signage abounds, identifying the plants and animals that call the region home. Together, they offer a unique experience in this well-maintained park.

The cavern near the start of the trail is popular with climbers on the weekend.

Left: The Pedernales River flows alongside a section of narrow, dusty trail.
Right: A rocky path leads up through the woods.

The hike starts with a scramble down into a narrow canyon peppered with ferns, white-flowered shrubby boneset, and Mexican sycamore. Chains on the walls will help you keep your footing. In a few more steps, the trail opens up to a wider but steep canyon valley as you pass trickling streams and a cavernous limestone grotto popular with climbers.

Stay to the left of the cavern floor as the trail leads you down a series of rocky steps before depositing you back on a narrow dirt path. At the bottom of this riparian canyon where a creek brings life and tall, limestone walls reach for the sky on either side, purple American beauty berry, Mexican buckeye, and other plants offer shade, but keep an eye out for poison ivy in warmer months.

There are several short trail offshoots in this area, but stay on the main path, following signs for the Upper River Trail and the way will soon open up to the Pedernales River. From here, find a spot to take a dip or continue on the rock and dirt riverside trail that will mostly be in full sun.

As you continue up and away from the river, picnic tables with a view of the river below are peppered under shady oaks from time to time.

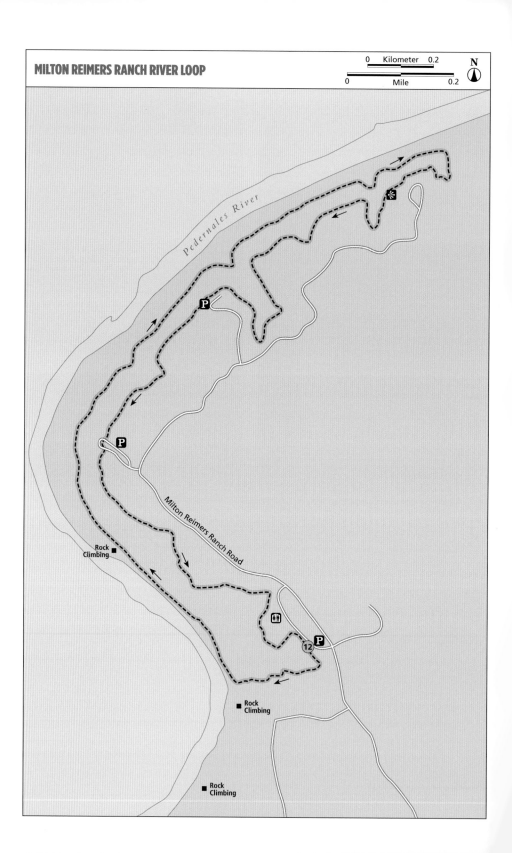

0   Kilometer   0.2

0   Mile   0.2

N

Pedernales River

Milton Reimers Ranch Road

Rock Climbing

Rock Climbing

Rock Climbing

12

At 1.9 miles, you'll head away from the river and into a shady wooded section where you'll ascend a steep, rocky slope with stone stairs before popping back into full sun in open grassland full of hearty plants adapted to survive the brutal Texas heat.

For the rest of the hike, follow the crushed granite path surrounded by Texas plants like Agarita, silverleaf nightshade with its tiny yellow berries, and cacti. From here on out it's an easy, mostly flat stroll along the plateau with views of the river through the foliage of live oak and cedar breaks flanked by dramatic limestone cliffs.

When you spot the parking lot and pavilion where you started your hike, know that all trails loop around and connect, but stay straight on the crushed granite trail that runs along the edge of the parking lot for the most direct route.

MILES AND DIRECTIONS

0.0 Start at the Climbers Canyon Trailhead.

0.1 At the first unmarked junction, descend straight down into the canyon.

0.1 Pass by the climbing grotto.

0.2 Continue on the trail that veers to the right at the Y-junction. Follow signs for Upper River Trail.

0.2 Go around the sideways tree to continue straight on the trail.

0.2 Turn left onto Upper River Trail and head down the stairs where the trail curves to the right.

0.3 Arrive at the Pedernales River. Trail continues to the right.

0.5 Continue straight on the Upper River Trail past the Back Door Exit sign.

0.7 The trail curves up a brief set of dirt and wood steps.

0.8 Continue straight following signs for Lower River Trail.

0.9 Continue straight across Lower River Trail parking and boat ramp. There are porta potties here.

1.0 Continue on the Lower River Trail to the right.

1.2 Go straight past the junction that leads to the River Bluff parking area.

1.3 Veer right following signs for Lower River Trail.

1.7 Veer left to stay closer to the river at what looks like a Y-junction with an unmarked trail.

1.9 Continue straight at the intersection, following signs for North Bank parking.

2.0 Turn right onto the narrow crushed granite path known as the Hike and Bike Trail.

2.0 Turn right to continue on the wide crushed granite path.

3.2 Cut across the paved cul-de-sac to continue onto the paved pathway on the other side.

3.6 Arrive at the overlook.

3.8 Take the trail that follows along the edge of the parking lot.

4.0 Arrive back at the trailhead and parking lot.

13 MULESHOE BEND RECREATION AREA GREAT ESCAPE TRAIL

This classic Texas Hill Country hike with varying terrain and plenty of Texas shade trees is mostly flat, easy, and popular with both hikers and mountain bikers. It's the perfect place for a leisurely stroll and to spot fields of bluebonnets in the spring.

Start: Great Escape Trailhead
Elevation gain: 692 to 812 feet
Distance: 6.3-mile loop
Difficulty: Easy due to mostly flat, largely shaded terrain
Hiking time: About 2.5 hours
Seasons/schedule: Year-round
Fees and permits: Day-use fee 13+ $5, children 12 and under free, seniors and disabled $2
Trail contacts: LCRA, PO Box 220, Austin, TX 78767; (512) 473-3366; https://www.lcra.org/parks/muleshoe-bend/
Canine compatibility: Dogs allowed
Trail surface: Dirt, rock
Land status: Lower Colorado River Authority (LCRA)

Nearest town: Spicewood
Other trail users: Mountain bikers
Maps: LCRA, https://www.lcra.org/download/muleshoe-bend-recreation-area-map-pdf/?wpdmdl=12725
Water availability: At park entrance
Special considerations: This is a popular mountain bike trail on weekends, so stay aware of your surroundings as you hike.
Amenities available: Restrooms, picnic tables, shelter, boat ramp, outdoor shower, camping
Maximum grade: 10% for 0.25 miles
Cell service: Cell service throughout

FINDING THE TRAILHEAD

From the park entrance, go approximately 250 feet to the trailhead parking lot, which will be on your left. **GPS:** 30.487290, -98.097960

Trail conditions: The dirt trail is intermittently sandy and rocky and usually only wide enough for one, though it occasionally broadens to several feet across. It is partially shaded throughout most of the hike, though there are a few brief sections in full sun.

THE HIKE

With almost 10 miles of single track and terrain that isn't too strenuous but will keep you on your toes, it's no wonder that Muleshoe Bend is a favorite among both hikers and mountain bikers. In fact, on weekends, you may find more visitors on two wheels than on two feet. But mostly shaded paths, a variety of trail surfaces, and an abundance of wildlife make the Great Escape Trail a picturesque hike any time of year.

It's also a very easy trail to follow. Metal signposts point you in the right direction at every junction and also feature trail distances so you can keep track of your progress. There are occasionally colored metal arrows on trees intended to guide you through tricky curving sections, which are abundant! But while there are many twists and turns, LCRA has done such a good job at maintaining and marking trails that it would be difficult to end up on a path you didn't intend to be on.

Top: A field of bluebonnets at Muleshoe Bend.
Bottom: Muleshoe Bend entrance.

Watch out for trip hazards like roots on the trail.

There aren't any aggressive inclines or declines to speak of—and the ones that do exist are fairly brief—but watch your footing, because large rocks and roots can create tripping hazards (but also make the trail interesting).

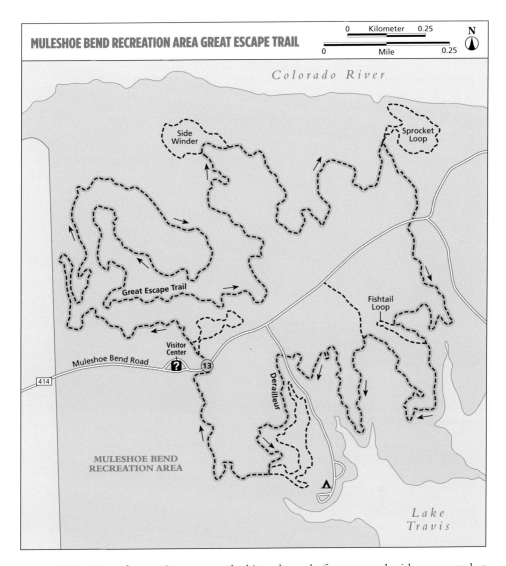

Colorado River

Side Winder

Sprocket Loop

Great Escape Trail

Fishtail Loop

Visitor Center

Muleshoe Bend Road

414

13

Derailleur

MULESHOE BEND RECREATION AREA

Lake Travis

Most times, the way is narrow and a bit rocky and often textured with tree roots, but there are also several sandy sections. There aren't many sweeping views along this trail, but there's plenty to look at: Grassland flanks the trail on either side in sunny stretches, and much of the trail is shaded by live oak trees and Ashe juniper with a smattering of Texas persimmon and the occasional yucca and prickly pear cactus, plus a pepper tree or two. Keep your eyes peeled and you'll also likely spot whitetail deer, lizards, and plenty of birds.

The trail is open and pleasant for hiking year-round thanks to the juniper trees that provide adequate shade, a welcome feature when Texas summer temperatures soar above 100. Bonus: After your hike, you can cool off in the Colorado River just a short drive down the park road! And in the spring, usually March and April, full fields of bluebonnets, Texas's state flower, color expansive swaths of waterfront parkland periwinkle and make for very popular photo ops.

Winding trails frequently lead through stands of Ashe juniper.

MILES AND DIRECTIONS

0.0 Start at the Great Escape Trailhead.

1.8 Continue on Great Escape Trail at the junction with the Recycler.

2.8 Keep straight on the trail past the next two junctions with Side Winder.

3.7 Cross a wide gravel road; the path is straight across on the other side. Continue on the trail past Sprocket Loop.

4.3 Continue past Fishtail Loop.

4.5 Spot the Colorado River on your left.

5.8 Continue straight past Derailleur.

6.3 Arrive back at the trailhead.

14 GRELLE RECREATION AREA WILD TURKEY AND OVERLOOK TRAIL

This mostly shaded trail offers enough elevation change to keep things interesting but not enough to wear you out, plus invites you to sunny viewpoints overlooking the Colorado River. Rocky, rolling terrain may offer a challenge for mountain bikers, but the variety simply adds spice for those traversing the park on foot among live oak and juniper.

Start: Wild Turkey Trail Trailhead
Elevation gain: 687 to 835 feet
Distance: 2.9-mile lollipop
Difficulty: Easy to moderate due to a few rocky, uneven sections and some ups and downs
Hiking time: 1.5 hours
Seasons/schedule: Year-round
Fees and permits: Day-use fee 13+ $5, children 12 and under free, seniors and disabled $2
Trail contacts: LCRA, PO Box 220, Austin, TX 78767; (512) 473-3366; https://www.lcra.org/parks/grelle/
Canine compatibility: Dogs allowed
Trail surface: Dirt and rock
Land status: Lower Colorado River Authority (LCRA)

Nearest town: Spicewood
Other trail users: Mountain bikers, horses
Maps: LCRA, https://www.lcra.org/download/grelle-recreation-area-map-pdf/?wpdmdl=12154
Water availability: None, so make sure to bring plenty
Special considerations: There is also camping available at this park if you care to spend more than an afternoon exploring the area.
Amenities available: Drop toilets located near the campground, camping, boating, swimming
Maximum grade: 10% for 0.5 miles
Cell service: Cell service throughout but may be weak in spots

FINDING THE TRAILHEAD

From the park entrance, follow the park road past scattered campsites. The lake will be on your left. Drive until the road dead-ends at a large gravel lot. The trailhead is at the far end. **GPS:** 30.480640, -98.139971

Trail conditions: Some sections of trail are narrow and rocky with brief ups and downs, sometimes with a bit of stair stepping, but the trail is mostly shaded. Other sections are wide and sunny but rocky.

THE HIKE

Another lovely park managed by LCRA, Grelle Recreation Area features the same well-marked, less-crowded trails as many of the parks under the organization's purview, most of which weaves through mature live oak trees with vast, reaching branches, Texas persimmon and Ashe juniper, plus prickly pear cactus and plenty of native grasses. And in the spring, patches of bluebonnets sprout along the trail (and over the hills near the trailhead).

Start out on Wild Turkey Trail, which is a shared trail for hikers and mountain bikers. The path is rocky and rolling with regular ups and downs that will get your heart pumping but that aren't prolonged. Some brief, steeper climbs do feature stair steps, but most are in blessed shade.

A few sections of the trail feature steps.

When the trail first splits, go left on Overlook Trail for a better view of Lake Travis where you might be able to spot white egrets posing along the waterfront.

When you reach the junction with Chaparral Run, veer left on Chaparral Run, which will lead you down toward the lake. During dry seasons, the water may be low, so don't expect to be able to dip your toes. If there's been a significant amount of rain during the season you're visiting, however, enjoy the views of the shimmering lake, which is part of the Colorado River.

Top left: Bluebonnets sprint along sections of trail and in fields near the trailhead in the spring.
Top right: A sunny section of trail flanked by Ashe juniper.
Bottom: A view of Lake Travis.

A hiker on Wild Turkey Trail.

The water is where the trail dead-ends, so after you snap a few photos and enjoy a snack, turn around to backtrack less than a tenth of a mile to start heading uphill on Chaparral Run, a wide, sunny, often uneven path that's shared by hikers, bikers, and horses. This section of trail features the longest incline and is in full sun, so pace yourself in the summer heat. On the upside, if you remember to turn around every once in a while, you'll be treated to frequent views of the lake behind you as you ascend.

When you reach the junction with Cottontail Loop at the top of the hill, turn right on a short connector trail dubbed Deer Track and enjoy an escape back into the shade created by abundant Ashe juniper trees and live oak.

In just a few steps, you will reach Cottontail Loop. There are no trail markers at this junction, but turn left. At the next junction, Cottontail Loop continues in what appears to be three directions, but turn right to head back toward Wild Turkey. Once you arrive, retrace your steps from the first 0.4 miles of the hike to return to the trailhead and treat yourself to a dip in the lake if you desire (just stay at least 50 feet from a boat ramp).

The entire park features a total of 8.3 miles of trails, many of which can be tacked onto this route to add anywhere from 0.1 to several miles. Alternatively, you can cut this loop short by sticking to just the Wild Turkey and Cottontail Loop Trails.

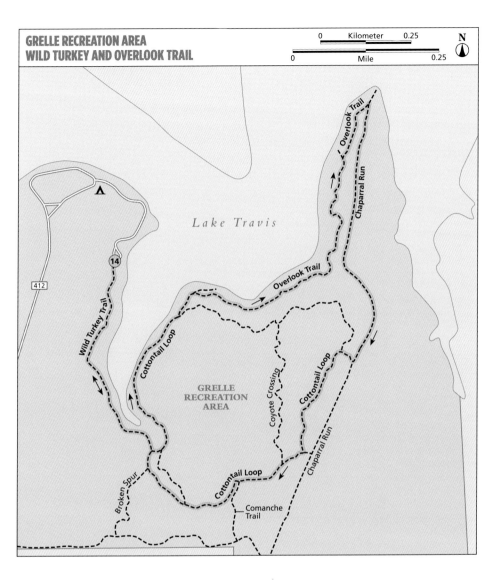

0   Kilometer   0.25

0   Mile   0.25

N

Lake Travis

GRELLE
RECREATION
AREA

Overlook Trail

Chaparral Run

Overlook Trail

Wild Turkey Trail

Cottontail Loop

Coyote Crossing

Cottontail Loop

Chaparral Run

Cottontail Loop

Broken Spur

Comanche
Trail

14

412

MILES AND DIRECTIONS

0.0 Start at the trailhead for Wild Turkey Trail.

0.4 Turn left on Cottontail Loop.

0.7 Veer left to continue on Overlook Trail.

1.3 Turn left onto Chaparral Run.

1.4 Reach the point, and turn around to head up the hill on Chaparral Run.

1.9 Turn right at the trail connecter for Cottontail Loop and continue left onto Cottontail Loop.

2.4 Continue straight onto Wild Turkey from Cottontail Loop.

2.9 Arrive back at trailhead.

15 PEDERNALES FALLS STATE PARK FALLS TRAIL

This trail may be short, but what it lacks in length it makes up for in picturesque views (and an opportunity to cool your feet on a hot day). While the falls may not be actively running if the area hasn't gotten rain in a while, there's always water in the multilevel pools, and the falls are always a beautiful place to relax and have a picnic.

Start: The Pedernales Falls parking lot at the very end of the park road
Elevation gain: 810 to 944 feet
Distance: 0.7-mile lollipop
Difficulty: Easy due to the short length of trail, but some steps are required
Hiking time: 30 minutes
Seasons/schedule: Year-round, park gates are closed from 10 p.m.–8 a.m.
Fees and permits: Day-use fee 13+ $6, children 12 and under free; reservations are recommended on weekends and holidays
Trail contacts: Pedernales Falls State Park, 2585 Park Rd. 6026, Johnson City, TX 78636; (830) 868-7304; https://tpwd.texas.gov/state-parks/pedernales-falls
Canine compatibility: On-leash only
Trail surface: Dirt, rock

Land status: Texas Parks and Wildlife Department
Nearest town: Johnson City, Dripping Springs
Other trail users: Mountain bikers
Maps: TPWD: Pedernales Falls State Park Trails map, https://tpwd.texas.gov/publications/pwdpubs/media/park_maps/pwd_mp_p4507_0026n.pdf
Water availability: Yes
Special considerations: There is no swimming in the falls. Also, on weekends and holidays, it's not a bad idea to make a reservation to visit this park.
Amenities available: Restrooms, water fountains
Maximum grade: 13% for 0.1 miles
Cell service: Spotty

FINDING THE TRAILHEAD

From the park entrance, drive down the main park road until it dead-ends at the Pedernales Falls Trail System parking lot. You will pass park headquarters where you will have to obtain a day-use permit. The trailhead will be at the far end of the parking lot loop. **GPS:** 30.334395, -98.252812

Trail conditions: The trail itself is intermittently wide and smooth and rocky and uneven. Several sections of stone steps must be navigated to reach the level of the falls. Most of the trail is in partial shade except for the area along the falls.

THE HIKE

Pedernales Falls is a popular state park not far from Austin, and for good reason: There are dozens of miles of trails, picturesque falls, swimming areas, and primitive camping. Naturally, this trail that leads to the dramatic rocky scenery of the falls themselves, a landscape carved by hundreds of years of erosion, is one of the most popular in the park. That's because there's plenty of opportunity to scramble and explore over rocks, enjoy the views, and on a sunny day, the pools perfectly reflect the brilliant blue of the Texas sky.

Top: The blue pools of Pedernales Falls from the overlook.
Bottom: The stone staircase and pathway to the falls.

A rocky trail near the falls.

There's no swimming in this section of the Pedernales River, but you can certainly dip your toes, take photos, and have a picnic in the shade. Swimming areas can be found farther downriver.

To get to the falls, you'll hike through a mostly shady section of juniper forest peppered with live oak. The trail starts out wide and mostly flat without many obstructions with only a gradual decline as you head to the first overlook.

Stay to the left when the trail forks at the beginning of the loop, following signs for Pedernales Falls Overlook. You'll return via the other side of this loop on the way back.

When you reach the upper overlook, read up on the history and geology of the area on the informational signs to your right, then take the man-made stone staircase down to the lower overlook. Take the stone steps on your left down toward the falls.

A staircase that leads back up to the overlook.

At the bottom of the stairs, you'll find a sandy beach area. Wander at your leisure over the exposed rocks and falls, but note that the opposite bank is private property, so stay off that side of the river. Listen to the water tumble over the smooth rock, and enjoy the views of pool after pool of blue-green water. Birds sing in the trees and green plant life like yucca, agarita, and juniper flourishes year-round.

You can return the way you came or continue downstream from the bottom of the stone staircase. A sandy, rocky path will lead you when water isn't exceptionally high. If it is, scramble over some of the large boulders until you reach a rocky riverbed surrounded by large rock limestone structures. This portion of the trail is in full sun, so come prepared.

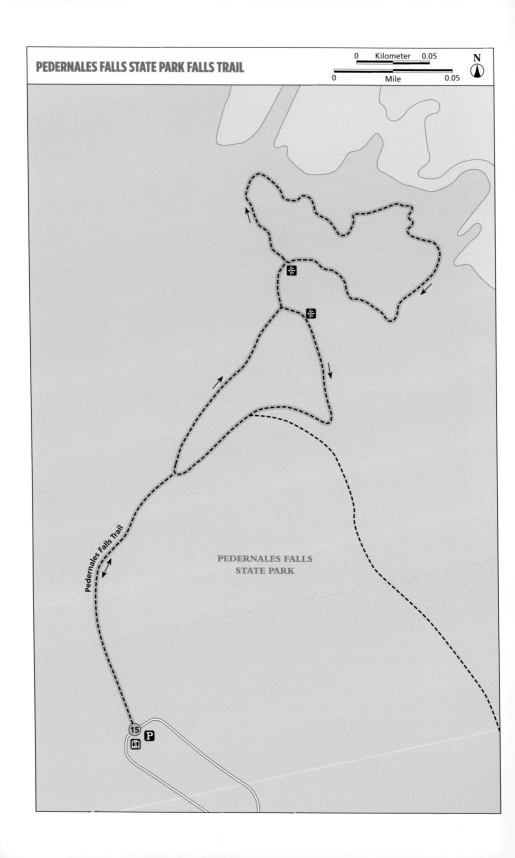

0   Kilometer   0.05

N

0   Mile   0.05

Pedernales Falls Trail

PEDERNALES FALLS
STATE PARK

15 P

Pedernales Falls.

When you reach the sandy bank on the other side, a narrow, rocky dirt trail just before you reach the beach will lead you back up toward the overlook. This section of trail is rough, uneven, and surrounded by juniper, so it's partially shaded, but it is not well-marked. Fortunately, it's clear and easy to follow. In just a few moments, you will reach another set of stone steps that lead you back up to the lower overlook.

Continue to your left up the stone steps to head back to the upper overlook and the main trail. When you reach the upper overlook, veer left to complete the loop. In another tenth of a mile, turn right at the intersection, following the sign for the parking lot. A few moments later, veer left where the initial loop split to return to the trailhead.

MILES AND DIRECTIONS

0.0   Start from the Pedernales Falls Trail System trailhead.

0.1   Veer left when the trail forks, follow signs for Pedernales Falls overlook.

0.2   Arrive at the upper overlook. Continue down the stone staircase to the left. Arrive at the lower overlook. Continue down the stone staircase to the left.

0.3   Reach a sandy beach area next to the falls, and turn right to walk along the riverbed.

0.4   Turn right onto the dirt path back toward the overlook.

0.5   Reach the lower overlook at the top of the stone stairs, and continue up. Reach the upper overlook, and turn left.

0.6   Turn right at the intersection. Following signs for the parking lot. Veer left toward the parking lot at the junction where the first loop splits.

0.7   Arrive back at the trailhead.

16 PEDERNALES FALLS STATE PARK MADRONE TRAIL AND JUNIPER RIDGE TRAIL

Meandering through dense juniper woods and along ridge lines, this rocky hike in one of Hill Country's most beloved parks offers a pleasant way to spend an afternoon and check off some miles before or after you visit the falls for which the park is named or take a dip in the river on a hot summer afternoon. The best thing about it: Unlike many trails in the area, this one is mostly shaded. What's more, it's frequently devoid of other hikers.

Start: The parking lot on Pedernales Falls Road; an informational sign with a map signals the start of the Madrone Trail

Elevation gain: 1,066 to 1,206 feet

Distance: 8.5-mile loop

Difficulty: Easy to moderate due to lack of elevation change and plenty of shade but long and with an uneven trail surface

Hiking time: 4 hours

Seasons/schedule: Year-round, park gates are closed from 10 p.m.–8 a.m. (This trailhead is outside park gates.)

Fees and permits: Day-use fee 13+ $6, children 12 and under free; reservations are recommended on weekends and holidays

Trail contacts: Pedernales Falls State Park, 2585 Park Rd. 6026, Johnson City, TX 78636; (830) 868-7304; https://tpwd.texas.gov/state-parks/pedernales-falls

Canine compatibility: On-leash only

Trail surface: Dirt, rock

Land status: Texas Parks and Wildlife Department

Nearest town: Johnson City, Dripping Springs

Other trail users: Mountain bikers

Maps: TPWD: Pedernales Falls State Park Trails map, https://tpwd.texas.gov/publications/pwdpubs/media/park_maps/pwd_mp_p4507_0026n.pdf

Water availability: Not at trailhead; only at park headquarters

Special considerations: On weekends and holidays it's not a bad idea to make a reservation to visit this park.

Amenities available: None

Maximum grade: 6% for 0.7 miles

Cell service: Spotty

FINDING THE TRAILHEAD

From the park entrance (you must obtain a day pass from the visitor center before hiking), turn left onto Pedernales Falls Road. Drive for 0.6 miles to a large gravel parking lot on the right side of the road. The trailhead is located at the far end of the lot. **GPS:** 30.280361, -98.246638

Make sure you also visit Pedernales Falls Trail (Hike 15) and take a dip in the swimming area before you leave the park. Primitive camping is also available in the park.

Trail conditions: The trail offers a variety of experiences, from mostly smooth dirt paths on the Madrone Trail to uneven, rocky, and narrow walkways through the trees. Mostly shaded, there are some brief sections of full sun and plenty of areas of exposed limestone, plus a view or two and the occasional creek crossing during wet seasons.

A sunny trail with big views.

THE HIKE

Of all the trails in Pedernales Falls State Park, this loop may be one of the least frequented, possibly because it is also the farthest from the namesake falls. As a result, you'll likely see few other hikers as you explore the miles of mostly shaded, rocky, and quiet trails.

The trailhead is technically outside of the gated entrance of the park, but you'll still need a day-use permit whether or not you made a reservation, so stop by headquarters before you hike to obtain one to put in your windshield.

Then, prepare to enjoy this winding loop that takes you through close juniper forest and a few open prairies. Along Madrone Trail, see if you can spot this unique tree with the same name, which stands out among typical Hill Country greenery thanks to its colorful, peeling bark. Depending on the time of year the bark may be red, orange, white, or brown with foliage that sprouts white flower clusters in the spring. You'll have to be vigilant, though, because while the tree may be the trail's namesake, they are few and far between.

What you will definitely spot are an abundance of Ashe juniper, live oaks, yucca, and prickly pear cactus, all of which lend a verdant hue to the trail year-round. In fact, sections of the trail feature such dense patches of juniper so close to the trail you may start to think of them as hiking companions.

As you hike, you will alternate between partially shaded juniper groves and sunny, open trail that permits views of big, blue Texas skies and the surrounding hills of the region.

A sunny and winding path.

Large chunks of limestone line sections of trail that is frequently just wide enough for one, especially along Juniper Ridge.

Juniper Ridge is named so because not only are there abundant juniper trees as far as the eye can see, but the trail also follows along a ridge line. Which means you get frequent views across hills and valleys as well as a fairly level (if rocky) route.

Keep your eyes peeled if you're hoping to spot wildlife; you may see deer, a variety of birds, even armadillos, though you will likely hear them before you see them (they are very loud diggers). Then enjoy the solitude and scenery on this lovely Hill Country hike.

Much of the trail is rocky and partially shaded.

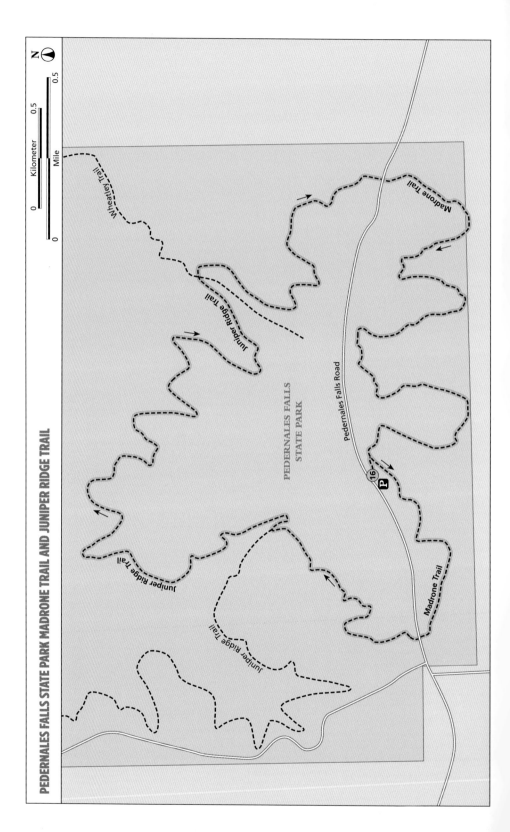

PEDERNALES FALLS STATE PARK MADRONE TRAIL AND JUNIPER RIDGE TRAIL

Wheatley Trail

Juniper Ridge Trail

Juniper Ridge Trail

Juniper Ridge Trail

PEDERNALES FALLS STATE PARK

Pedernales Falls Road

Madrone Trail

Madrone Trail

N

Kilometer

0   0.5

0   0.5
Mile

Left: A shaggy juniper along a partially shaded trail.
Right: An armadillo digs for dinner.

MILES AND DIRECTIONS

0.0 Start from the trailhead parking lot on Pedernales Falls Road. Continue past the informational sign onto the sunny trail under the power lines.

0.1 At the junction with Madrone Trail, turn right. In a few more steps, veer right onto Madrone Trail.

0.9 Cross Pedernales Falls Road and continue onto Madrone Trail on the other side.

1.7 Turn right onto Juniper Ridge Trail.

2.6 Veer left, following signs for Juniper Ridge Trail at the intersection with Horse Trail.

3.9 Cross a gravel service road and continue on Juniper Ridge Trail on the other side.

4.8 Continue straight across the intersection with Wheatley Trail.

5.8 Turn right at Madrone Trail (east entrance).

6.0 Cross Pedernales Falls Road to continue on Madrone Trail.

8.4 Arrive back at the beginning of the loop, turn right on the connector trail to the trailhead, and follow the path as it curves to the left toward the parking lot.

8.5 Arrive back at the trailhead and parking lot.

17 BALCONES CANYONLANDS VISTA KNOLL TRAIL

Located within the Warbler Vista Unit of Balcones Canyonlands, this partially shaded loop with winding paths and rolling ups and downs offers lots of variety when it comes to trail surface and views and is just challenging enough to keep you on your toes. And the wildlife refuge designation means there's plenty of opportunity to spot wildlife, including, if you're lucky, the endangered golden-cheeked warbler that nests in the area in the summer.

Start: Cactus Rocks Trailhead
Elevation gain: 997 to 1,269 feet
Distance: 2.1-mile loop
Difficulty: Moderate due to rocky trails and some elevation change
Hiking time: 1 hour
Seasons/schedule: Best in spring or fall but open year-round from sunrise to sunset
Fees and permits: None
Trail contacts: Balcones Canyonlands National Wildlife Refuge, 24518 E. FM 1431, Marble Falls, TX, 78654; (512) 339-9432; https://www.fws.gov/refuge/balcones-canyonlands
Canine compatibility: No pets allowed
Trail surface: Dirt, rock
Land status: US Fish and Wildlife Services National Wildlife Refuge
Nearest town: Lago Vista

Other trail users: Hikers only
Maps: US Fish and Wildlife Services, https://www.fws.gov/refuge/balcones-canyonlands/map, Friends of Balcones Canyonlands National Wildlife Refuge https://www.friendsofbalcones.org/hiking
Water availability: No water available at trailhead
Special considerations: This hike can be very hot in the summer, and there's no water at the trailhead, so bring plenty. Also, due to the presence of endangered species no speakers are permitted on trails.
Amenities available: Restrooms at the trailhead
Maximum grade: 13% for 0.2 miles
Cell service: Cell service available throughout

FINDING THE TRAILHEAD

 From FM 1431, turn right onto Warbler Vista. Drive up the park road to the Warbler Vista parking lot at the Cactus Rocks Trailhead. The trailhead is located across the park road from the parking lot. **GPS:** 30.505619, -97.979741

Trail conditions: The partially shaded trail features both wide dirt paths and narrow rocky passages. It's partially shaded at times but just as often in full sun.

THE HIKE

Located in one of two main units of Balcones Canyonlands National Wildlife Refuge (four if you count the location of the headquarters just down the road and a viewing deck north of the Doeskin Ranch Unit), Warbler Vista offers approximately 4 miles of hiking trails through protected lands. Located on the Edwards Plateau, two bioregions meet here to create a rich tapestry of flora and fauna, the most famous resident being the endangered golden-cheeked warbler.

In fact, that bird, together with the black-capped vireo, which was recently removed from the threatened species list, are part of the reason the 1,000-acre refuge exists: to

A rocky trail is partially shaded in the late afternoon.

Top: Juniper and live oak offer partial shade on sections of trail.
Bottom left: The shaggy bark of the iconic Ashe juniper.
Bottom right: A signpost for Vista Knoll Trail.

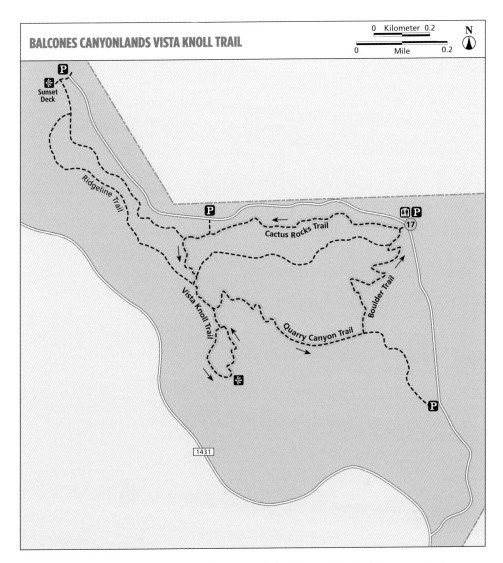

preserve prime nesting and breeding grounds for these and other birds, namely, the seemingly endless breaks of juniper trees, the only trees in which the endangered birds nest.

Which is why on any given weekend, especially in the spring and summer, you'll see plenty of people wandering trails with binoculars and cameras. The refuge even hosts a songbird festival in the spring.

Birds aside, when you're ready to hike, grab a map at the information sign at the trailhead and start down the Cactus Rock Trail. Just a few steps in, turn right toward a short set of rock steps to start hiking counterclockwise around the loop. You'll immediately be surrounded by a forest of Ashe juniper. Also prickly pear cactus, Mexican buckeye, cedar sedge, and Spanish oak. But even with all the greenery, expect only partial shade on this trail that transitions from dirt to rocky limestone and back again many times.

As you venture on, there won't be any colored trail markers or blazes painted on trees, but the path is clear, stacked rock cairns occasionally guide the way, and there are directional signs at every intersection, making the route, which takes you from Cactus Rocks Trail to Vista Knoll Trail to Quarry Canyon Trail to Boulder Trail, easy to follow.

Along the way, expect intermittent sections of partial shade and full sun. Meaning in the summer, bring a hat, sunscreen, and plenty of water. The Vista Knoll Trail especially is sunny and exposed, but it offers plenty of opportunity to appreciate the surrounding landscape and roadway below (and unfortunately, construction on a new development). You can also spot the curving Colorado River winding between the hills in the distance.

By the time you connect to Quarry Canyon Trail, road noise dissipates as the path rolls up and down juniper-blanketed hills, and birdsong abounds. Holly and Texas persimmon punctuate the trailside as the path ascends as you head back toward the trailhead.

MILES AND DIRECTIONS

0.0   Start from the Cactus Rocks Trailhead.

0.0   A few steps later, turn right up a short set of rock steps to hike the loop counterclockwise.

0.5   Veer left to stay on Cactus Rocks Trail at the junction with a parking lot connector trail.

0.6   Continue straight on Cactus Rocks Trail.

0.7   Turn left onto Vista Knoll Trail.

0.7   Follow signs to the left for Vista Knoll Trail.

0.8   At the junction with Quarry Canyon Trail and Vista Knoll Trail, veer right to continue on the loop portion of Vista Knoll Trail.

1.1   Arrive back at the start of Vista Knoll Trail Loop. Veer right to head back to the junction with Quarry Canyon Trail.

1.2   Turn right onto Quarry Canyon Trail.

1.6   Turn left on Boulder Trail.

2.0   Turn right onto Cactus Rocks Trail toward the parking lot.

2.1   Arrive back at the trailhead.

18 BALCONES CANYONLANDS INDIANGRASS TRAIL

Wide-open prairie, juniper forest, shallow creeks, and an abundance of plant life—and wildlife—make this park and trail system a gem among Hill Country hikes. Bring your binoculars if you hope to spot birds like the endangered golden-cheeked warbler, or simply wander the series of trails and take in the miles-long views of the area and see how many kinds of dragonflies, trees, or wildflowers you can identify. Take note that this trail is located within the Doeskin Ranch Unit of Balcones Canyonlands.

Start: The Doeskin Ranch Trailhead
Elevation gain: 1,063 to 1,311 feet
Distance: 3.3-mile loop
Difficulty: Moderate due to some rocky paths and full sun
Hiking time: 1.5 hours
Seasons/schedule: Best in spring or fall but open year-round from sunrise to sunset
Fees and permits: None
Trail contacts: Balcones Canyonlands National Wildlife Refuge, 24518 E. FM 1431, Marble Falls, TX, 78654; (512) 339-9432; https://www.fws.gov/refuge/balcones-canyonlands
Canine compatibility: No pets allowed
Trail surface: Dirt, rock
Land status: US Fish and Wildlife Services National Wildlife Refuge
Nearest town: Liberty Hill
Other trail users: Hikers only

Maps: US Fish and Wildlife Services, https://www.fws.gov/refuge/balcones-canyonlands/map; Friends of Balcones Canyonlands National Wildlife Refuge, https://www.friendsofbalcones.org/hiking
Water availability: No water available at trailhead
Special considerations: This hike can be very hot in the summer as large portions are fully exposed. There's no water at the trailhead, so bring plenty. Also, due to the presence of endangered species, no speakers or trail running are permitted.
Amenities available: Restrooms down the hill from the trailhead at the main trail hub; there is occasionally a mobile ranger unit in the parking lot
Maximum grade: 15% for 0.2 miles
Cell service: Spotty at best

FINDING THE TRAILHEAD

 From FM 1174 or Mountain Creek Road, turn right into the Doeskin Ranch parking lot. The trailhead and information sign are located in the corner of the parking lot. **GPS:** 30.620944, -98.074314

Trail conditions: This trail is largely in full sun, though there are sections of partial shade, and features wide dirt paths, narrow rocky passages, and creek crossings that may require you to get your feet wet in rainy seasons.

THE HIKE

Located in the rolling hills northwest of Austin, Balcones Cayonlands National Wildlife Refuge offers a quiet respite in nature. The Doeskin Ranch Trailhead unit is one of several within the preserve system, and probably the most popular, though on weekdays you may only spot a handful of cars in the parking lot at most.

Expect gradual, sunny inclines as you hike.

Along the trail, thickets of oak offer the perfect home for the black-capped vireo and the reason this area was originally designated a preserve in 1992. But it's also home to the endangered golden-cheeked warbler, hence the area's designation as a Globally Important Bird Area. Bring your binoculars or zoom lens if you hope to spot one.

This sunny hike meanders over a variety of landscapes and trails, including the Rimrock Trail, Shin Oak Trail, and Indiangrass Trail. Because the route is made up of three separate loops, you have the option to shorten your hike by taking just the first two loops or you can add on an additional 0.6 miles by hiking Creek Trail in addition to Indiangrass Loop.

As you hike, you'll wander through partially shaded sections of live oak and juniper, sunny prairies dotted with wildflowers like mountain pink in the spring and summer, and sections of delightfully verdant riparian creekside greenery like buttonbush and sycamore trees. Sugar hackberry, Texas persimmon, and mustang grape flank trails, live oak offers shade, and prairie flameleaf sumac pops up in patches between tall, yellow-green grasses.

The main trail hub is located just a few steps down the trail where several trails begin in earnest. At this point, continue straight onto the sunny gravel path as you follow signs for Rimrock Trail.

After spending some time walking in the sun, the trail ascends and descends over rocky limestone hills through partially shaded juniper forest that offer a brief respite from the heat, but watch your footing as the trail is rocky and uneven and diamondback rattlesnakes call the preserve home.

Take note that this trail is located within the Doeskin Ranch unit of Balcones Canyonlands (there are several other units within Balcones Canyonlands).

Top: There are a few welcome partially shaded sections along the way.
Bottom: The view from a high point on Indiangrass Trail Loop.

A creek crossing on Indiangrass Trail Loop.

Shin Oak Trail and Indiangrass Trail lead you up and around wide-open prairie plateaus where you'll spot plenty of prickly pear cactus, sumac, yucca, and a variety of grasses, plus miles-long views of Hill Country. The landscape may appear sparse, but there is an abundance of life here.

After completing the Indiangrass Loop and turning right onto Shin Oak Trail, you'll crest a short hill and come back down the other side and turn right to continue on Rimrock Trail, reentering partial shade and following signs for the parking lot.

After you cross the creek at 3.1 miles, continue up the path to the next junction with Creek Trail and Rimrock Trail and continue straight up the white gravel path back toward the parking lot. When you reach the main trail hub with the bathrooms and informational sign, return the way you came up the paved path toward the parking lot.

BALCONES CANYONLANDS INDIANGRASS TRAIL

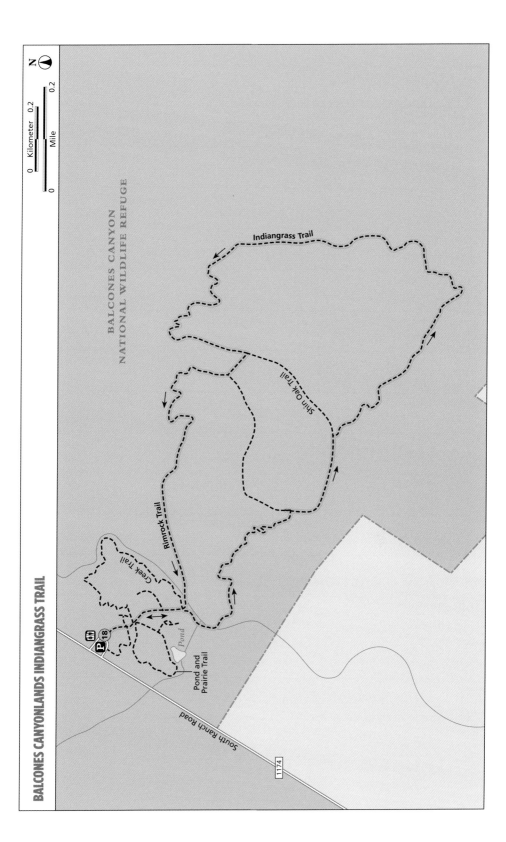

BALCONES CANYON
NATIONAL WILDLIFE REFUGE

Indiangrass Trail

Shin Oak Trail

Rimrock Trail

Creek Trail

Pond and
Prairie Trail

Pond

South Ranch Road

1174

N

0   Kilometer   0.2

0   0.2
Mile

A sunny path on Indiangrass Trail Loop.

MILES AND DIRECTIONS

0.0 Start at the informational sign at parking lot trailhead and walk down the paved path.

0.1 Continue straight onto the gravel path following signs for Rimrock Trail.

0.2 At the junction with Creek Trail, continue straight onto Rimrock Trail.

0.7 Turn right at the junction onto Shin Oak Trail.

0.9 Turn right onto Indiangrass Trail.

2.4 At the junction, turn right onto Shin Oak Trail.

2.5 Veer right onto Rimrock Trail.

3.1 Cross the creek and continue straight onto the gravel path at the junction with Creek Trail and Rimrock Trail to head back toward the parking lot.

3.3 Arrive back at the trailhead parking lot.

19 INKS LAKE STATE PARK LOOP TRAIL (PECAN FLATS TRAIL, CONNECTING TRAIL, WOODLAND TRAIL, LAKE TRAIL)

This sunny hike features shimmering lake views, tiny cacti, and big granite. Landscapes rarely get more colorful than this in Hill Country, nor more sun-soaked. So bring plenty of water and sun protection and don't forget to make time to cool off in the lake after you're done!

Start: Pecan Flats Trailhead
Elevation gain: 892 to 1,012 feet
Distance: 4.7-mile lollipop
Difficulty: Moderate due to rocky terrain and exposed trail
Hiking time: 2 hours
Seasons/schedule: Year-round, open daily 8 a.m.–10 p.m.
Fees and permits: Day-use fee 13+ $7, children 12 and under free
Trail contacts: Inks Lake State Park, 3630 Park Rd. 4 West, Burnet, TX 78611; (512) 793-2223; https://tpwd.texas.gov/state-parks/inks-lake
Canine compatibility: On-leash only
Trail surface: Dirt, rock
Land status: Texas Parks and Wildlife (Texas State Park)

Nearest town: Burnet
Other trail users: Hikers only
Maps: TPWD, https://tpwd.texas.gov/publications/pwdpubs/media/park_maps/pwd_mp_p4507_0015v.pdf
Water availability: Fountains located at the restroom building nearby
Special considerations: This trail has limited shade; it can get extremely hot in the summer.
Amenities available: Restrooms, picnic tables, and trash cans not at trailhead but at park entrance and down the park road
Maximum grade: 15% for 0.3 miles
Cell service: Throughout

FINDING THE TRAILHEAD

From the park entrance gate, drive straight ahead to the amphitheater parking lot. An informational sign with a map marks the beginning of the Pecan Flats Trail. **GPS:** 30.736851, -98.370181

Trail conditions: The trail is intermittently sandy dirt and solid rock. Most of the trail is in full sun and can be hot in the summer.

THE HIKE

Subtle rises and falls, a variety of terrain, and big lake views (plus plenty of lake activities) make Inks Lake a supremely popular destination for residents of Austin and Hill Country. In fact, the park campground is often booked to capacity on weekends weeks in advance from spring through fall.

The lake, perfect for fishing, swimming, and kayaking, draws many, but the hiking is just as stunning, as are the very stones you walk on. In fact, part of

> Just down the road is Longhorn Cavern State Park. The cave is only accessible via guided tour but offers a cool (literally) underground look at some of the area's history—geological and otherwise.

A view of Inks Lake from a high point in the trail.

what makes this part of Hill Country so unique is the pinkish granite that colors the landscape. This ancient gneiss (pronounced "nice") is not only easily identifiable by its rosy hue, but it's also what the Texas State Capitol building is made of. In fact, those stones were quarried and transported from just down the road in Marble Falls.

And there's plenty of it to marvel at as you hit the trail. Surrounded by juniper, live oak, and plenty of prickly pear and Christmas cholla cactus, spiky green yucca, and Texas persimmon, the well-marked and maintained trail varies between sandy and wide to narrow and rocky. At lower points in the trail, and closer to the water line of the lake, riparian zones are resplendent with life. But atop short climbs over rocky trails, rock covered with lichen sparkle in the sun.

The trail, where you'll start on a wide, partially shaded gravel and dirt path before the trail enters an open field where you'll climb in elevation, often over granite hills, starts on the partially shaded Lake Trail, identified be green markers. It then transitions to Pecan Flats Trail (yellow markers). At 0.7 miles, at the Y-junction, veer right to stay on the inner loop of Pecan Flats Trail. You can continue straight around the back half of the loop if you'd like to add 0.5 miles to your route.

Pink granite boulders cover the landscape.

At 1.2 miles, the Pecan Flats loop meets with the red Connecting Trail. Continue toward the Woodland Trail where you'll ramble among native plants like Indian blanket and cacti. The trail will roll in easy ups and downs and if you pay attention, you may even spot tiny, furry fleece hedgehog cactus.

At 3.6 miles, the trail will split at a Y junction where you will veer left and cross the road. The Woodland Trail will continue straight across on the other side and connect to Lake Trail.

Take the loop to the left to enjoy big lake views. Hop around on the large granite boulders before you head back down on the rocky trail where you'll continue to get an eyeful of Inks Lake.

INKS LAKE STATE PARK LOOP TRAIL (PECAN FLATS TRAIL, CONNECTING TRAIL, WOODLAND TRAIL, LAKE TRAIL)

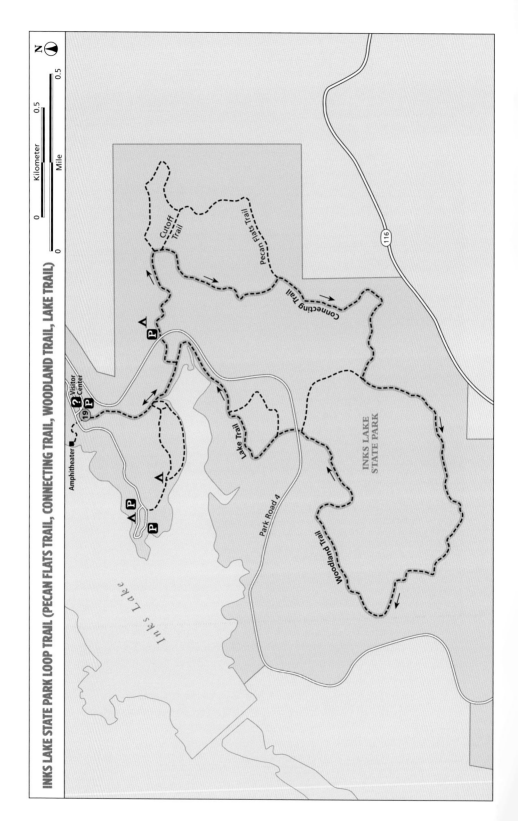

Left: Rocky, sunny trails are the norm on this hike.
Right: Yucca and prickly pear cacti are not in short supply at Inks Lake.

Continue on Lake Trail until you return to the trailhead at 4.7 miles. Then enjoy a swim at the beach just down the park road. You earned it.

MILES AND DIRECTIONS

0.0 Start from the Lake Trail Trailhead in the amphitheater parking lot.

0.2 At the junction, continue straight to stay on Lake Trail, marked with blue arrows.

0.4 Veer left onto Pecan Flats Trail, marked with yellow arrows.

0.5 Cross the road. The trail continues directly across on the other side past the red gate.

0.7 At the junction, turn right to stay on the inner loop of Pecan Flats Trail.

1.2 Turn right on the red-blazed Connecting Trail.

1.8 Continue to the left where the Connecting Trail dead-ends at the blue-blazed Woodland Trail.

3.6 At the Y-junction, turn left and cross the roadway. Woodland Trail will continue straight across on the other side.

3.7 Woodland Trail meets Lake Trail, marked with green trail markers.

4.3 At the junction, turn left to continue on Lake Trail.

4.5 Continue right to stay on Lake Trail.

4.7 Arrive back at the trailhead.

20 INKS LAKE STATE PARK DEVIL'S WATERHOLE AND VALLEY SPRING CREEK TRAIL

Multiple water access points and long views of Valley Creek make this short but picturesque hike a welcome wander on hot summer days, a lovely loop to complete in between watching swimmers leap from the cliffs at Devil's Waterhole. It's especially suitable for adventurous wanderers keen to scurry up limestone climbs for striking views and scamper down the rocks to the waterfalls and clear pools below.

Start: Devil's Waterhole Trailhead
Elevation gain: 892 to 971 feet
Distance: 1.4-mile lollipop
Difficulty: Easy to moderate due to the short length but several steep climbs and large step-ups
Hiking time: 45 minutes
Seasons/schedule: Year-round, open daily 8 a.m.–10 p.m.
Fees and permits: Day-use fee 13+ $7, children 12 and under free
Trail contacts: Inks Lake State Park, 3630 Park Rd. 4 West, Burnet, TX 78611; (512) 793-2223; https://tpwd .texas.gov/state-parks/inks-lake
Canine compatibility: On-leash only
Trail surface: Dirt, rock

Land status: Texas Parks and Wildlife (Texas State Park)
Nearest town: Burnet
Other trail users: Hikers only
Maps: TPWD, https://tpwd.texas.gov/ publications/pwdpubs/media/park _maps/pwd_mp_p4507_0015v.pdf
Water availability: At the restrooms
Special considerations: There are several swimming holes along the way, so bring your swimwear and sunscreen.
Amenities available: Restrooms, picnic tables, trash cans
Maximum grade: 18% for 0.1 miles
Cell service: Throughout

FINDING THE TRAILHEAD

From the park entrance gate, take the main park road to your right and follow signs for Devil's Waterhole on the twisting park roads. There is a parking lot at the trailhead, but it fills quickly on weekends. Additional parking is located around the campground. An informational sign is posted at the start of the trail, a wide, paving stone-lined dirt and gravel path. **GPS:** 30.745718, -98.360552

Trail conditions: The trail is intermittently sandy dirt, rocky soil, and stone. Most of the trail lacks shade and is hot in the summer, making the frequent water access points all the more welcome in warmer months.

THE HIKE

When planning a hike in a park named for a body of water, you expect there to be frequent access points to said water. This trail does not disappoint in that regard. In fact, this short, quick trail makes for a perfect midafternoon hike after you've tackled one of the park's longer trails (like Hike 10) and are ready to find a place to cool your feet or take a dip.

After walking down the hill from the trailhead, you'll cross a footbridge in short order. At this point, you'll start to see a few areas off to your left where you can set up a camp chair or a hammock and relax in the shade by the lake. But before you do, continue down the trail to the right toward Devil's Waterhole, which you'll find at the 0.2-mile

Top: Swimmers climb on the limestone cliffs at Devil's Waterhole.
Bottom: The creek and its various swimming holes flow and pool in the pink granite.

Devil's Waterhole offers an excellent and picturesque place to take a dip.

mark. Here, a small shady cove offers a place to sit and relax or slide into the water for a swim and watch the adrenaline junkies leap off the rocks into the water just across the narrowing lake.

After you pass the waterhole, head up the granite hill straight ahead to start on the Valley Spring Creek Trail. At the top of the short, steep climb, scramble up the boulders to your left for impressive views of the lake that turns into Valley Spring Creek below before continuing down the dirt path. Follow the green and white dots painted on the rock that mark the route. But don't be afraid to wander to the edge of the granite cliffs to get a view of the creek below, and, often, access to the creek itself, including at a small waterfall.

It won't likely be flowing if there hasn't been rain recently, but if water levels are high, a lovely cascade flows over the water-eroded limestone. At any time of year, pools of water

The clear water of Valley Creek.

teem with life and feed a lush, green riparian environment along the creek bed and the banks. On either side, pink granite cliffs peppered with prickly pear cactus, live oak, and juniper flank the creek.

At around the 0.7-mile mark, the trail meets up with the Devil's Backbone Nature Trail, which, if taken, can extend your hike an additional 1.2 miles each way. Turn right to head back toward Devil's Waterhole on the Valley Spring Creek Trail. The return loop will be farther from the creek with fewer viewpoints, but you will get small sections of shade in exchange.

At 1.2 miles, find yourself back at Devil's Waterhole. Take a dip, enjoy the refreshing lake, or retrace your steps on the Devil's Waterhole Trail back to the trailhead and parking area, and enjoy the abundant Christmas cholla and prickly pear cactus, live oak, and honey mesquite along the way.

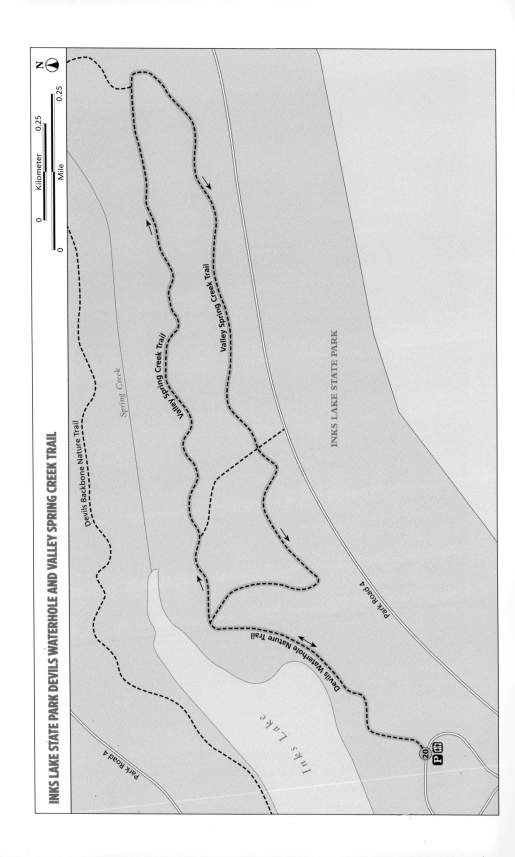

INKS LAKE STATE PARK DEVILS WATERHOLE AND VALLEY SPRING CREEK TRAIL

N

Kilometer
0   0.25

Mile
0   0.25

Spring Creek

Devils Backbone Nature Trail

Valley Spring Creek Trail

Valley Spring Creek Trail

INKS LAKE STATE PARK

Park Road 4

Devils Waterhole Nature Trail

Inks Lake

Park Road 4

20

The dirt path is frequently in full sun.

MILES AND DIRECTIONS

0.0   Start at Devil's Waterhole Trailhead.

0.2   Arrive at Devil's Waterhole and the beginning of Valley Spring Creek Trail. Continue straight up the granite field.

0.3   Stay on the trail to the left with the green and white bullseye painted on the rock.

0.7   The trail runs into Devil's Backbone Nature Trail. Turn right to stay on Valley Spring Creek Trail and complete the loop.

1.2   The trail reconnects with Devil's Waterhole Trail. Turn left and retrace your steps to the trailhead.

1.4   Arrive back at the trailhead.

Want to extend your hike? Tack on the Devil's Backbone Trail, an out-and-back trail that will add 1.2 miles onto your route each way. It offers views of the lake from the opposite bank and ends at a large bird blind with a small amphitheater for excellent birdwatching.

21 REVEILLE PEAK RANCH DECISION POINT LOOP

Unparalleled views await at this stunning park that consists of nearly 100 kilometers of trails, all of which are open to hikers and mountain bikers. Shade, sunshine, creek crossings, forested and rocky landscapes, plus plenty of wildlife—including wild boars—all combine to make this long hike one of the true underappreciated shining jewels of Hill Country.

Start: The main trailhead on the far end of the parking lot
Elevation gain: 996 to 1,280 feet
Distance: 9.0-mile double lollipop
Difficulty: Moderate due to some rises and falls, and one steep climb
Hiking time: 4 hours
Seasons/schedule: Open year-round, trails closed until noon on Thurs
Fees and permits: Day-use fee 12+ $10, children 6–11 $5, children 5 and under free; cash or check only
Trail contacts: Reveille Peak Ranch, 105 CR 114, Burnet, TX 78611; (512) 914-9411, (512) 755-1177; https://www.rprtexas.com/
Canine compatibility: Dogs allowed

Trail surface: Dirt, rock
Land status: Privately owned
Nearest town: Burnet
Other trail users: Mountain bikers and hikers
Maps: Reveille Peak Ranch map, https://www.rprtexas.com/trails
Water availability: At the pavilion
Special considerations: This is also an event center and hosts obstacle races some weekends, so check the calendar before you go: https://www.rprtexas.com/events.
Amenities available: Restrooms, picnic tables, shelter, showers
Maximum grade: 10% for 1.5 miles
Cell service: Cell service throughout

FINDING THE TRAILHEAD

From the park entrance on Little Midland Dorbandt Road (right off Ranch to Market Road 2341), drive down the gravel road until you reach the large, open parking area next to the pavilion. The trailhead will be at the far end to the right of the pond and pavilion. **GPS:** 30.800521, -98.334054

Trail conditions: The trail offers a wide variety of hiking surfaces and terrain, from wide, packed-dirt jeep roads to narrow rocky footpaths to fields of granite. A good portion of it is in full sun.

THE HIKE

Reveille Peak Ranch is a relatively undiscovered Hill Country gem, at least among hikers. While it's slightly more popular among mountain bikers, trails only opened to hikers during the pandemic, and thank goodness, because there are scores of miles to explore. While you may encounter a mountain biker from time to time on weekends, they're nearly nonexistent on weekdays, thanks in part to the sheer number of routes available.

Start your hike to the right of the pavilion and pond on a jeep road next to a sign that points toward the trailhead proper (think of the jeep road as an access road). Loop around the far end of the pond and enjoy the wide, sunny trail surrounded by silverleaf nightshade, prickly pear cactus, juniper, honey mesquite, and lichen-covered granite boulders.

Top: Pools of water at Decision Point.
Bottom: A yucca plant along a trail of pink granite.

A creek crossing along the Beginner Trail.

Continue until you reach the trailhead gate at 1.1 miles where there is a painted map and a list of trails and their color signatures. Go straight to start on the blue Beginner Trail, a narrow, often shady, occasionally rock-strewn path that offers sporadic views of the surrounding hills and valleys as you traverse the many brief rises and falls in elevation.

You'll encounter many trail junctions as you hike, but most are well-marked with color-coded trail markers in the form of spray-painted PVC pipe. If you do end up on the wrong one, don't panic—almost all of them converge again at some point. Just don't get too distracted by the ever-changing landscape—occasionally populated by free-roaming cattle—as wooded sections of trail open up to boulder fields and green cacti, blue sky, and reddish dirt.

At 2.8 miles, join the Jeep trail again very briefly before veering back to the left onto the blue Beginner Trail. At 3.6 miles, cross the creek by hopping between large granite rocks that break through the water's surface.

A mother cow and calf along the trail.

At 3.8 miles, arrive at the junction with Decision Point Trail, which is identified by green markers. Turn right and hike up. At the top, a sign announces your arrival and a stone pathway leads to a chapel-like setup with rows of wooden benches and a rustic wooden cross, all surrounded by pools of water formed by erosion in the granite.

Enjoy the stunning 360-degree views, including Lake Buchanan in the distance. In the hours before sunset, a golden glow washes everything in warm light and casts deep shadows on boldly illuminated rock faces and natural structures jutting out of the landscape. Greens, pinks, reds, and plenty of blue make for stunning views.

Turn around and retrace your steps back down the hill toward the Beginner Trail and turn right when you reach the junction. More pink granite colors the trail and the landscape on this side of the park. Continue on the Beginner Trail as it twists and turns, pass through the Pipe Gate that's marked on the map around 7.4 miles, and find yourself back at the Trailhead Gate at about 7.8 miles.

Camping for tents and RVs is also available at Reveille Peak Ranch, and sites are usually available. Entry fees are payable via cash or check only.

Turn right onto the jeep road and walk it all the way back to the parking area.

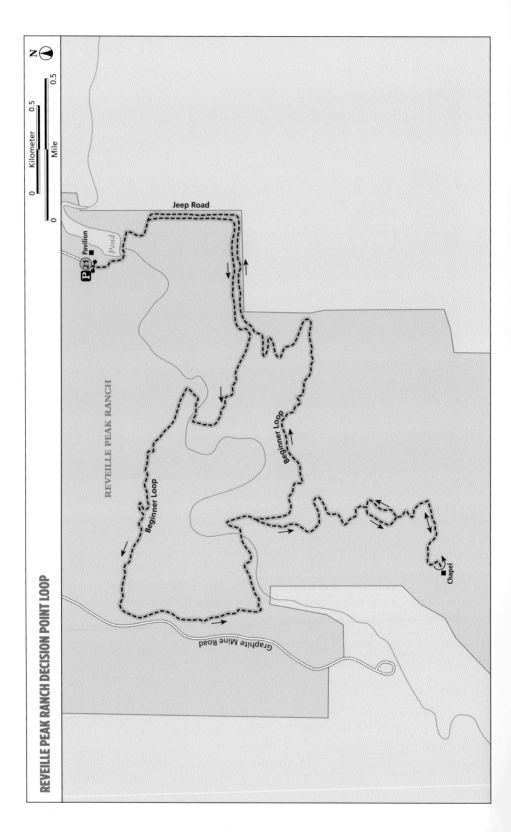

REVEILLE PEAK RANCH DECISION POINT LOOP

N

Kilometer
0   0.5

Mile
0   0.5

Pavilion

P (21)

Pond

Jeep Road

REVEILLE PEAK RANCH

Beginner Loop

Beginner Loop

Graphite Mine Road

Chapel

The cross at Decision Point.

MILES AND DIRECTIONS

0.0 Start at the trailhead at the beginning of the jeep road and follow it until you reach the Trailhead Gate.

1.1 Enter the trail system through the gate, continue straight onto the Beginner Trail with a blue marker.

1.5 Continue straight across the junction to continue on the Beginner Trail.

1.6 Continue straight across the junction to continue on the Beginner Trail.

2.1 Pause at a viewpoint.

2.6 Beginner Trail curves right and then left across a series of intersections.

2.8 Join the Jeep trail briefly, then veer to the left onto Beginner Trail.

2.9 Continue straight across the intersection. Stay on Beginner Trail.

3.3 Cross the Jeep trail. Continue on Beginner Trail to your left.

3.6 Cross the creek.

3.8 Turn right on the Green Trail to Decision Point.

5.1 Reach Decision Point. Turn around and head back down.

6.3 Turn right at the junction with Beginner Trail.

6.8 Veer right to stay on Beginner Trail.

7.1 Continue straight on Beginner Trail.

7.4 Pass through the Pipe Gate.

7.6 Cross several junctions, staying on Beginner Trail.

7.8 Arrive back at the Trailhead Gate, turn right on the jeep road to retrace your steps to the parking lot.

9.0 End at the parking lot trailhead.

22 CANYON OF THE EAGLES LAKESIDE TRAIL LOOP

This wide, quiet trail offers plenty of opportunities to spot wild-life and enjoy a walk with friends. It's a leisurely stroll that curves between sun and shade and leads along the edge of Lake Buchanan. Many days, you can expect to have the trail entirely to yourself. It's the perfect place for company but also a meditative solo ramble with several access points to the lake.

Start: Amphitheater Trailhead near the RV campground
Elevation gain: 1,021 to 1,079 feet
Distance: 3.0-mile circuit
Difficulty: Easy thanks to mostly flat, wide paths
Hiking time: 1.5 hours
Seasons/schedule: Year-round
Fees and permits: Day-use fee 8+ $10; $5 for seniors, first responders, and veterans; children 7 and under free; free for guests of the resort
Trail contacts: Canyon of the Eagles, 16942 Ranch Rd. 2341, Burnet, TX 78611; (512) 334-2070; https://canyonoftheeagles.com
Canine compatibility: On-leash only
Trail surface: Dirt
Land status: Lower Colorado River Authority Park (LCRA) operated by Canyon of the Eagles

Nearest town: Burnet
Other trail users: Hikers only
Maps: Canyon of the Eagles, https://canyonoftheeagles.com/PDFs/Menus/TrailMap2021.png?_t=1637963328
Water availability: At campground across the park road
Special considerations: Your entrance fee is good for the whole day, so after your hike, you can also visit the on-site restaurant, swim in the lake, take a guided nature walk, or stay late and book a star program at the Eagle Eye Observatory (for an additional fee).
Amenities available: Restrooms, picnic tables, and showers across the resort road
Maximum grade: 8% for 0.3 miles
Cell service: Throughout

FINDING THE TRAILHEAD

From the park entrance station, turn left and drive down the resort road for 0.5 miles. The signposted Amphitheater Trailhead parking lot will be on your right. **GPS:** 30.8812530, -98.4378001

Trail conditions: The trail is occasionally narrow and gravelly, but overall it is smooth, wide, and flat and easily accommodates two or more hikers walking abreast. There is little to no shade on much of the trail, so in the summer, it's recommended that the hike be done early in the day.

THE HIKE

Located in Canyon of the Eagles, a sprawling nature-based park and resort, this preserve and trail system are comanaged by the Lower Colorado River Authority, so even if you're not staying at the picturesque Hill Country property, you can still purchase a day-use pass to explore the area, including the Lakeside Trail that offers plenty of opportunity to spot birds and other wildlife as well as enjoy views of Lake Buchanan.

This trail is one of the only loops in the preserve that's open year-round; many are closed from March 1 to August 31 for the endangered golden-cheeked warbler and

The late afternoon sun shines through the trees above the dirt path.

Canyon of the Eagles is also a resort and campground, complete with guest rooms, tent and RV sites, camp store, kayak rentals, and frequent events. Book a stay to immerse yourself in nature and explore all of the property's 16 miles of trails, or visit the on-site restaurant, swim in the lake, take a guided nature walk or family-friendly wildlife presentation, or stay late and make reservations for the star program at the Eagle Eye Observatory (for an additional fee).

A sunny view of Lake Buchanan from the trail.

black-capped vireo nesting season. It also perfectly accommodates slow, leisurely strolls with friends and binocular-wielding birders. No part of it is difficult or technical, most of the trails are wide to encourage conversation, and the scenery and wildlife help round out an easy, enjoyable walk.

The trail itself is well-marked and maintained with signage at all junctions (and many bends in the trail), all identified with a number in a circle that corresponds to the trail junction on the map, which you can pick up in the welcome office or at the entrance station. Signs also point you in the direction of the next junction, making it easy to locate yourself on the map.

Start at the amphitheater trailhead on the fairly broad dirt path toward Rocky Point Trail. The path is wide enough to accommodate two, even three people in some places, though it does narrow in a few sections. As you hike, peer through the Texas persimmon, yucca, and juniper nearest the trail toward the fields of prickly pear cacti and the surrounding Hill Country terrain, complete with granite outcroppings that step down in dramatic affect toward the valley below.

At 0.5 miles, you'll arrive at a small lookout on Tanner Point, the first of several lake viewpoints. Here, the trail becomes grassy and is flanked by hundreds of prickly pear cacti that blanket the landscape like wildflowers. Short footpaths occasionally lead down to the lake that, on sunny days, reflects the same blue as the sky.

At 0.7 miles, you will transition to Lakeside Trail and be surrounded by honey mesquite trees that offer a few moments of shade. Be on the lookout for deer, lizards, birds, rabbits, and other wildlife as you walk.

When you reach signpost 8 at 1.1 miles, continue on Lakeside Trail or take the trail to the left to hike to Reflection Point, which will add an additional 0.4 miles to your

Trees offer partial shade at best along sections of the trail.

trip. This will lead you toward the lake and ends at a large grassy area with lake access on either side of the narrow peninsula. Wander down to the beach to dip your toes, set up a blanket and have a picnic, and then head back the way you came.

At 2.2 miles, at junction marker 11, hang a right onto Beebrush Loop to start heading back to the parking lot through slightly more tree cover thanks to abundant juniper.

CANYON OF THE EAGLES LAKESIDE TRAIL LOOP

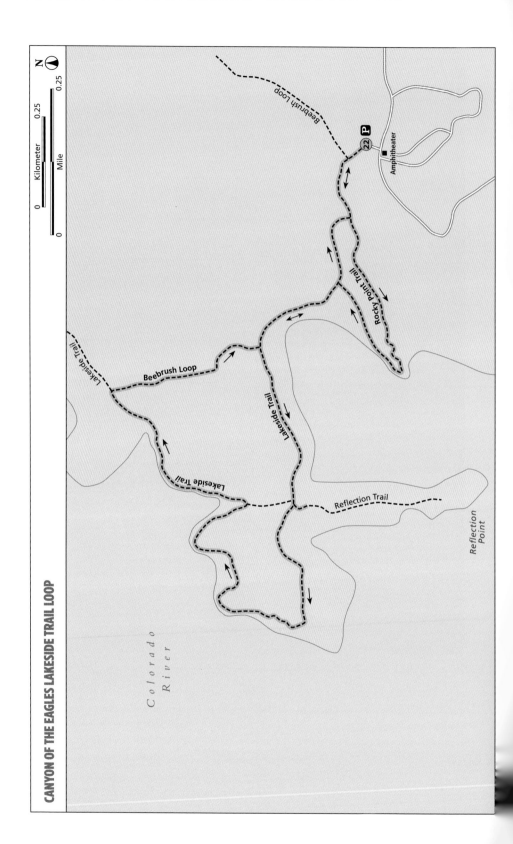

N

0   Kilometer   0.25

0   0.25
                        Mile

Beebrush Loop

Lakeside Trail

Beebrush Loop

Rocky Point Trail

22 P

Amphitheater

Lakeside Trail

Lakeside Trail

Reflection Trail

Reflection Point

Colorado River

Prickly pear cacti, a frequent sight along the trail.

MILES AND DIRECTIONS

0.0 Start from the Amphitheater Trailhead and take the trail to the left.

0.1 Pass through the gate and a sign commencing the start of the trail. Continue straight toward Rocky Point.

0.2 Arrive at trail junction 4. Continue straight to stay on Rocky Point Trail.

0.5 Junction marker 5 directs you to the right.

0.7 At junction 6, turn left to head to junction 7 toward Lakeside Trail.

0.8 Reach junction 7 and continue straight toward junction 8.

1.1 Arrive at signpost 8 and go straight toward signpost 9. Optional: Take the trail to the left to walk to Reflection Point to add 0.4 miles to your trip.

1.4 The trail curves to the right at junction marker 9.

1.8 Reach junction marker 10. Veer left to complete the Lakeside Trail loop.

2.2 Turn right onto Beebrush Loop at marker 11 to hike toward marker 7.

2.5 Arrive back at junction marker 7 and continue toward marker 6, retracing your steps on this section of trail for 0.2 miles.

2.7 Veer left at marker 6 to continue on Beebrush Loop toward marker 4.

2.8 At junction marker 4, turn left to retrace your steps from the first 0.2 miles back to return to the Amphitheater Trailhead.

3.0 Arrive back at the trailhead.

23 COLORADO BEND STATE PARK SPICEWOOD SPRINGS TRAIL AND SPICEWOOD CANYON TRAIL

If it's a scenic hike you're after that offers a plethora of opportunities to sit, rest, and take a cooling dip during the long, hot summer, this trail will not disappoint. One side of the loop will have you rambling over rocks, across streams, and past natural springs, while the other leads you up to dramatic overlooks in partially shaded forest. In between: shady woods populated with towering trees and plenty of shade.

Start: Spicewood Canyon Trailhead
Elevation gain: 1,023 to 1,232 feet
Distance: 4.1-mile lollipop
Difficulty: Moderate due to frequently rocky terrain and some elevation change
Hiking time: 2 hours
Seasons/schedule: Year-round, park hours are 6 a.m.–10 p.m.
Fees and permits: Day-use fee 13+ $5, children 12 and under free
Trail contacts: Colorado Bend State Park, PO Box 118, Bend, TX 76824; (325) 628-3240; ColoradoBendSP@tpwd.texas.gov, https://tpwd.texas.gov/state-parks/colorado-bend
Canine compatibility: On-leash only
Trail surface: Dirt, rock
Land status: Texas Parks and Wildlife Department (Texas State Park)
Nearest town: Lampasas

Other trail users: Mountain bikes permitted on Spicewood Canyon Trail only
Maps: TPWD maps https://tpwd.texas.gov/publications/pwdpubs/media/park_maps/pwd_mp_p4507_0140n.pdf
Water availability: Water is available at the campground near park headquarters
Special considerations: There is little to no cell service after you head down the park road from the entrance gate, so download any offline maps you need before entering the park.
Amenities available: Restrooms, picnic tables, and snacks nearby at park headquarters; boat ramp in the trailhead parking lot
Maximum grade: 15% for 0.5 miles
Cell service: No cell service

FINDING THE TRAILHEAD

From the park entrance station, drive down the park road to park headquarters, then turn right on the gravel road. It dead-ends at a day-use area with a parking lot and boat ramp on your left. The trailhead is at the far end of the lot. **GPS:** 31.017966, -98.448217

Trail conditions: The trail starts out wide, sunny, and flat on smooth packed dirt, but much of the trail is rocky and uneven with several sections of cliffside trail, tall limestone step-ups, and rough trail surfaces. Much of the trail is in at least partial shade.

THE HIKE

The crowning jewel of this popular hike in Colorado Bend State Park is the series of springs and pools that emanate from underground aquifers. Small waterfalls and verdant

A small waterfall along the creek.

riparian ecosystems flourish on the banks, and on hot summer days, the welcoming pools tempt hikers to sit, soak, and cool down toward the beginning or end of their hike.

Indeed, the hike can be done in either direction, but these directions lead you clockwise.

The trail starts off on a shady, level dirt path that quickly transitions to full sun, peppered with interpretive signs that highlight local flora and fauna. Wildflowers, lush grasses, and mature live oak trees, American sycamore, and black willow flank the trail and obscure the view of the Colorado River to your left.

Water cascades over rock at one of many small waterfalls.

At 0.4 miles, continue straight to stay on Spicewood Springs Trail at the junction with Spicewood Canyon Trail. In a few more steps, a shady grove with a picnic table and a small foot path down to the river are located on the left, but turn right at the red trail marker that points the way up and over a small ridge to the first spring.

An overlook offers a view of the creek below.

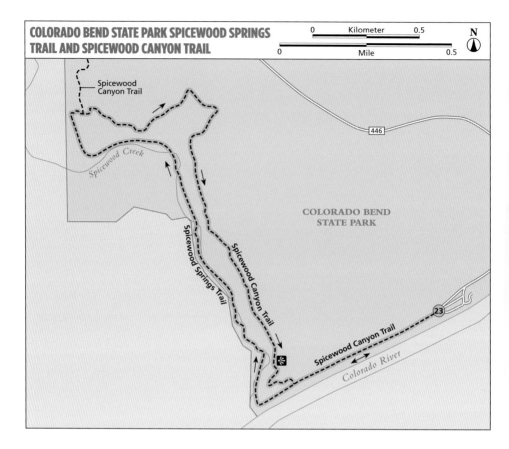

COLORADO BEND STATE PARK SPICEWOOD SPRINGS TRAIL AND SPICEWOOD CANYON TRAIL

Spicewood
Canyon Trail

446

COLORADO BEND
STATE PARK

Spicewood Creek

Spicewood Springs Trail

Spicewood Canyon Trail

23

Spicewood Canyon Trail

Colorado River

Kilometer

Mile

0   0.5

N

Here, water cascades in a series of small falls into pools of varying depths. Ferns, native grasses, and vines cover the rocks and banks surrounding the springs, a welcome oasis on a hot summer day. In the crystal clear water of the upper pools, watch fish swim in circles.

Take a dip if you're keen, then cross the creek, following blue blazes and trail markers. Soon, the trail starts to slowly climb in elevation on a rocky, exposed path with large step-ups and -downs as the foliage changes from ferns to Ashe juniper and yucca.

You'll continue to cross the creek at intervals, but after doing so around 1.1 miles, the trail continues up the limestone toward the top of the cliffs surrounding the pool. Here, the trail transitions to a shady, forested setting with tall, mature juniper and live oak.

At the 2.0-mile mark, you'll reach the junction with Spicewood Canyon Trail. Turn right here to head back to the trailhead via the Canyon Trail. Trail markers will now be red instead of blue and the trail is rocky and uneven and mostly shaded, though it pops into sunny sections between Texas persimmon, prickly pear cactus, and squat juniper at times.

Around 2.9 miles, and again at 3.4, pause at the lookout points to the right of the trail for views of Gorman Creek below, then start heading back down as the trail descends into the valley.

When the Spicewood Canyon Trail dead-ends at Spicewood Springs Trail, turn left to retrace your steps on the 0.4 miles of open, sunny path that you started on and take it all the way back to the trailhead.

Rocky outcroppings next to one of the many springs.

MILES AND DIRECTIONS

0.0 Start at the Spicewood Canyon Trailhead.

0.4 Continue straight at the junction with Spicewood Canyon Trail and Spicewood Springs Trail.

0.6 Find a shady grove with a picnic table, turn right at the red trail marker, and arrive at the first spring.

2.0 Turn right at the junction with Spicewood Canyon Trail.

2.9 Stop at the lookout point.

3.4 Stop at the second lookout point.

3.6 Turn left onto Spicewood Springs Trail.

4.1 Arrive back at the trailhead.

24 COLORADO BEND STATE PARK GORMAN FALLS TRAIL AND TIE SLIDE TRAIL

This sunny hike navigates rocky terrain on the way toward an expansive lookout perched high on the cliffs overlooking the Colorado River, followed by a descent to the geologically unique Gorman Falls. Along the way, expect plenty of native flora and a chance to dip your toes or cool off in the Colorado River or a nearby spring, a chance to refresh yourself after miles of sunny, rocky trails.

Start: Gorman Falls Trailhead
Elevation gain: 1,022 to 1,328 feet
Distance: 4.8-mile reverse lollipop
Difficulty: Moderate due to heat in the summer, very rocky, uneven terrain, and an exceptionally steep, slippery descent to the falls
Hiking time: 2.5 hours
Seasons/schedule: Year-round, park hours are 6 a.m.–10 p.m.
Fees and permits: Day-use fee 13+ $5, children 12 and under free
Trail contacts: Colorado Bend State Park, PO Box 118, Bend, TX 76824; (325) 628-3240; ColoradoBendSP@ tpwd.texas.gov, https://tpwd.texas .gov/state-parks/colorado-bend
Canine compatibility: On-leash only
Trail surface: Dirt, rock

Land status: Texas Parks and Wildlife Department
Nearest town: Lampasas
Other trail users: Hikers and mountain bikers
Maps: TPWD, https://tpwd.texas.gov/ publications/pwdpubs/media/park _maps/pwd_mp_p4507_0140n.pdf
Water availability: Water is only available at the campground near park headquarters at the far end of the park
Special considerations: Cell service is spotty, and the trail is exposed and can get very hot in the summer. Bring adequate sun protection and water.
Amenities available: Restrooms
Maximum grade: 25% for 0.1 miles
Cell service: Spotty throughout

FINDING THE TRAILHEAD

From the park entrance, drive 0.3 miles down the park road to the very first trailhead parking sign on your left. Drive down the gravel road to the parking lot and trailhead at the end. **GPS:** 31.058333, -98.501201

Trail conditions: Tie Slide Trail is narrow and rocky with minor elevation changes and limited shade. Gorman Falls Trail features large slabs of uneven limestone over much of the trail, even less shade, and a short, steep, rocky descent to the falls.

THE HIKE

Toward the northern edge of Texas Hill Country sits popular Colorado Bend State Park, a true respite from city life just 2 hours from Austin. With miles and miles of hiking and biking trails, primitive and developed campsites, and abundant wildlife like deer and armadillos, it's an excellent place to spend a day or a whole weekend. And if it's views and unique geology you're looking for, this trail will not disappoint.

As you begin, Tie Slide Trail is just as often closely flanked by Ashe juniper and young live oak trees as it is in full sun, which makes it a hot trek on sunny summer days. But

Unique calcium deposits at the falls.

follow blue trail markers and you'll venture from cedar breaks to bright clearings where you can see for miles over the tops of pale yucca and prickly pear cactus.

At 1.5 miles, continue straight on Tie Slide past the junction that points toward Gorman Falls Trail and travel over rocky downhill terrain for 0.1 miles to reach the lookout, also known as Rusty's Roost. Here, you'll find a wooden platform and sweeping views of the Colorado River below as it winds to the north and southeast. The platform itself

Top: A view of the Colorado from high above as enjoyed from the overlook.
Bottom: Several sections of trail are rocky and uneven.

is in full sun, but there are a few spots of partial shade in the trees nearby where you can sit, rest, and refuel.

To continue, turn around and head 0.1 miles back to the last intersection. Veer left, following signs that direct you to Gorman Falls Trail. At 2.4 miles, Tie Slide Trail will dead-end into orange-blazed Gorman Falls Trail. Turn left and enjoy a change in scenery: Here, large slabs of relatively flat but uneven limestone make up the sunny path.

A sunny view along the trail.

Over the last 0.8 miles toward the falls, the trail will descend and intersect with several additional trails, but continue toward Gorman Falls. At 3.3 miles, the trail gets steep as it descends atop limestone boulders, which are often slippery, especially when wet. Fortunately, there is a wire to hold onto as you work your way down (and then back up).

There are more than a dozen trails in Colorado Bend, so stay a while and explore or reserve a campsite for a few days.

At the bottom, you'll find a shady viewing platform with benches that offer a place to rest and appreciate the unique falls, which are covered in travertine, formed by the buildup of calcium in the water that pours from above. The process is very similar to the formation of stalactites and stalagmites in underground caves but here more closely resembles green-gray curtains made of stone.

Swimming near and touching the falls aren't allowed, but there are several very short paths that lead down to the river so you can dip your feet in the Colorado. Alternatively, below and behind the observation deck, near where the falls meet the river, there is a spring with clear, clean water that is perfect for a refreshing dip.

When you're ready to head back, turn around and retrace your steps up the steep limestone cliff. When you reach the junction with Tie Slide Trail, continue straight to stay on Gorman Falls Trail and take it all the way back to the trailhead.

MILES AND DIRECTIONS

0.0 Start from the Gorman Falls Trailhead and take Tie Slide Trail to the left.

1.5 Continue straight at the junction that points you toward Gorman Falls Trail.

1.6 Arrive at the Colorado River overlook (Rusty's Roost).

COLORADO BEND STATE PARK GORMAN FALLS TRAIL AND TIE SLIDE TRAIL

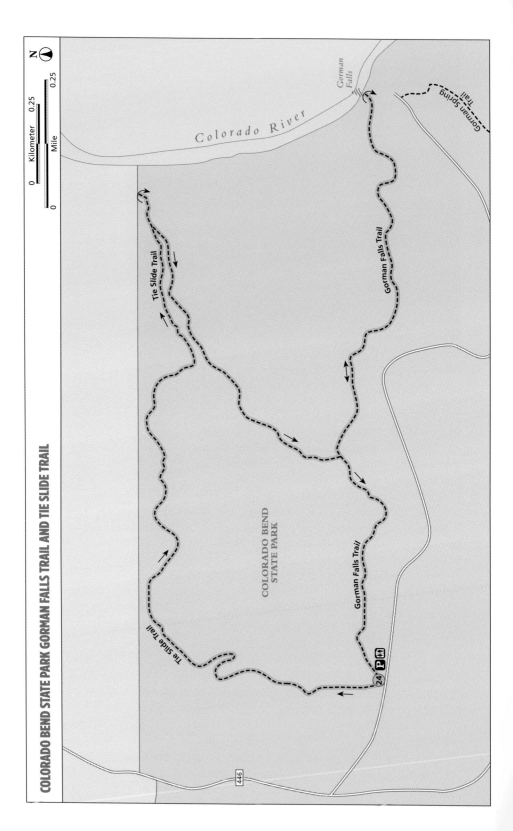

A spring bubbles out of the earth's surface below the falls.

1.8 Arrive back at the junction that points you toward Gorman Falls Trail and veer left.

2.4 Turn left onto Gorman Falls Trail.

3.1 Veer left to continue toward Gorman Falls at the junction with Gorman Falls Trail and the bicycle route to Gorman Spring.

3.2 Turn left at the junction of Gorman Falls Trail and trails that lead to Gorman Creek and Spring.

3.4 Reach Gorman Falls.

3.7 Arrive back at the junction with the Gorman Creek and Spring Trail. Turn right on Gorman Falls Trail.

4.4 Continue straight on Gorman Falls Trail past the junction with Tie Slide Trail.

4.8 Arrive back at the trailhead.

25 ENCHANTED ROCK SUMMIT TRAIL

Enchanted Rock, as the name implies, is a special place. And the most magical (and popular) hike in this state natural area is the famous Summit Trail that leads you to the top of the massive rock itself. Part of the trail is made up of zigzagging rock steps and dirt paths, but most of it is an unmarked climb up the smooth pink granite surface of the massive batholith. Almost the entire trek is uphill (and then back down again), but the expansive views at the top and the surprisingly abundant vernal pools filled with native flora and fauna at the summit make it more of a thrill than a challenge.

Start: Summit Trail Trailhead
Elevation gain: 1,398 to 1,816 feet
Distance: 1.3-mile out-and-back
Difficulty: Difficult due to the steep climb to the top
Hiking time: 1 hour
Seasons/schedule: Open year-round, though the most pleasant time to visit is spring when flowers bloom and everything is green; park hours are 6:30 a.m.–10 p.m. daily (gate closes at 8:30 p.m.)
Fees and permits: Day-use fee 13+ $8, children 12 and under free
Trail contacts: Enchanted Rock State Natural Area, 16710 Ranch Rd. 965, Fredericksburg, TX 78624; (830) 685-3636; https://tpwd.texas.gov/state-parks/enchanted-rock
Canine compatibility: Dogs are not permitted on the summit trail (they are allowed on the Loop Trail and in the campground area)
Trail surface: Granite, packed dirt
Land status: Texas State Parks and Wildlife
Nearest town: Fredericksburg
Other trail users: Hikers only
Maps: TPWD, https://tpwd.texas.gov/publications/pwdpubs/media/park_maps/pwd_mp_p4507_119q.pdf
Water availability: At the visitor center entrance station and at the bathrooms beside the parking lot
Special considerations: This trail is in full sun and can be extremely hot in summer. Bring adequate water and sun protection.
Amenities available: Restrooms, picnic tables, water fountains
Maximum grade: 20% for 0.4 miles
Cell service: Cell service throughout

FINDING THE TRAILHEAD

From the park visitor center, make two lefts and a right to head toward the upper parking lot by the gazebo. You can also park in the lower lot and extend your hike by just 0.1 miles. **GPS:** 30.498273, -98.818888

Trail conditions: The trail is fully exposed for the entirety of the hike and the trail itself is almost entirely on the granite dome that is Enchanted Rock. The slope isn't slippery, but it is steep.

THE HIKE

Think of Enchanted Rock—the structure, not the park—like a glacier: What you see is only a fraction of the mass that exists underground. But when the natural structure in question is a rock—in this case pink granite—instead of frozen water, it's called a batholith. And it makes for an imposing structure in the Hill Country landscape with an underground structure that spans over 100 square miles beneath the surface.

The vernal pools on top of Enchanted Rock.

From the top, there are no better views of Hill Country. You'll be treated to 360-degree vistas and access to a number of vernal pools, often lined with greenery and home to rare species like tiny fairy shrimp. These singular ecosystems develop in depressions in the rock and are extremely delicate, so stay out of the water.

Start your hike at the Summit Trailhead by the upper parking lot near the bathrooms and picnic area. Fill up your bottles because it can be hotter at the summit than at the base thanks to the rock absorbing and radiating heat from the sun. Then head toward two red-roofed shade structures where you will find informational signs and displays about the park and the geographic landscape and head down the dirt and wood steps to begin in earnest on the Summit Trail, a dusty path on a bed of granite that's surrounded by Ashe juniper, prickly pear cactus, and agarita, among other native plants.

The path will narrow and start going up. Follow the yellow arrows on signposts and ascend the many series of steps carved into the pink granite.

At around 0.3 miles, the trail will start to smooth out and you'll begin ascending a fairly steep but smooth section of rock dome. Make your way over and around the large rock formations and continue to follow the yellow arrows toward the summit.

By 0.6 miles you'll arrive at the top. It's a large, wide-open space, so wander around, peer into the vernal pools, see if you can spot the miniature shrimp, and find all of the nooks and crannies and boulders to scramble across. You can see for miles in every direction and there will likely be a kettle of turkey vultures surfing thermals nearby.

Once you've fully explored, turn around and head back down the way you came.

It's a good idea to make reservations in advance if you plan to visit the park on weekends or holidays. The park is extremely popular and often fills to capacity by morning.

Top: The trail leading to Enchanted Rock.
Bottom: Hikers rest at the top of Enchanted Rock and take in the view.

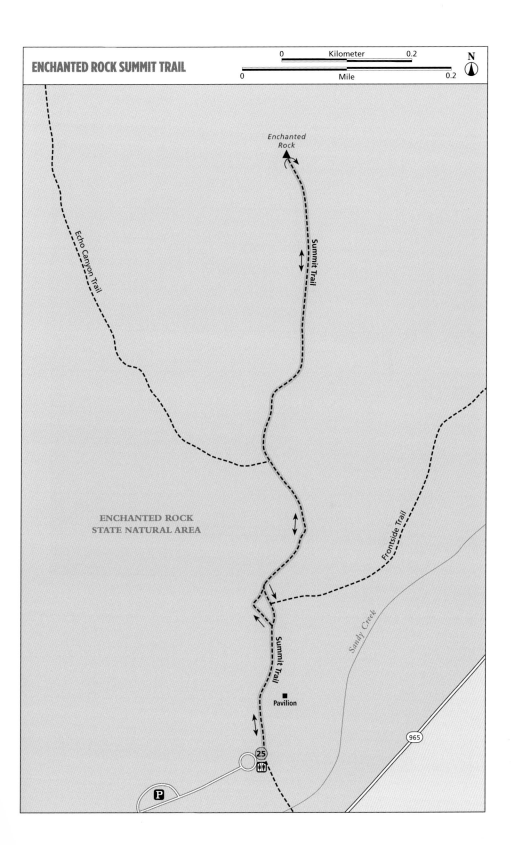

ENCHANTED ROCK SUMMIT TRAIL

Kilometer
0   0.2

Mile
0   0.2

N

Enchanted
Rock

Echo Canyon Trail

Summit Trail

ENCHANTED ROCK
STATE NATURAL AREA

Frontside Trail

Sandy Creek

Summit Trail

Pavilion

965

25

P

Prickly pear cactus blossom.

MILES AND DIRECTIONS

0.0 Start from the Summit Trail Trailhead at the far end of the upper parking area near the bathrooms and picnic area.

0.1 Arrive at the pavilion and overlook. Informational signs explain the history and geology of the area.

0.1 Veer slightly left following signs for Summit Trail.

0.3 Begin ascending straight up a fairly steep, smooth section of granite.

0.6 Reach the summit. Explore. Turn around and head down the way you came.

1.3 Arrive back at the small pavilion. Continue to the official trailhead and parking lot.

1.3 Arrive at the trailhead and parking lot.

26 ENCHANTED ROCK LOOP AND ECHO CANYON TRAIL

While the Summit Trail might be the crowning jewel of this park, if you want to escape the crowds, examine massive granite structures from a different angle, or simply take a longer walk around the park, this trail is an excellent option. You can even tack on the top portion of the summit trail to the end of this hike if you haven't completed it already. But on this path, you'll meander by lakes, between domes, and scramble up rocky canyons. If you skip the Echo Canyon portion of the trail and complete the whole loop instead, you can even bring your pup along for the hike!

Start: Loop Trail Trailhead
Elevation gain: 1,355 to 1,601 feet
Distance: 4.2-mile loop
Difficulty: Moderate due to a mostly level path but full sun and uneven terrain
Hiking time: 2.5 hours
Seasons/schedule: Open year-round, though the most pleasant time to visit is spring when flowers bloom and everything is green; park hours are 6:30 a.m.–10 p.m. daily (gate closes at 8:30 p.m.)
Fees and permits: Day-use fee 13+ $8, children 12 and under free
Trail contacts: Enchanted Rock State Natural Area, 16710 Ranch Rd. 965, Fredericksburg, TX 78624; (830) 685-3636; https://tpwd.texas.gov/state-parks/enchanted-rock
Canine compatibility: Dogs are permitted on the Loop Trail and in the campground area but not on Echo Canyon Trail
Trail surface: Rock, packed dirt
Land status: Texas State Parks and Wildlife
Nearest town: Fredericksburg
Other trail users: Hikers only
Maps: TPWD, https://tpwd.texas.gov/publications/pwdpubs/media/park_maps/pwd_mp_p4507_119q.pdf
Water availability: At the visitor center entrance station and at the bathrooms beside the parking lot
Special considerations: This trail is in full sun for most of the way and can be extremely hot in summer. Bring adequate water and sun protection.
Amenities available: Restrooms, picnic tables, water fountains
Maximum grade: 15% for 0.2 miles
Cell service: Cell service throughout

FINDING THE TRAILHEAD

From the park visitor center, head to the right toward the lower parking area. The trailhead is located at the end of the roundabout.
GPS: 30.497352, -98.817986

Trail conditions: Most of this trail is in full sun. There are frequent ups and downs over intermittently rocky and dusty terrain, and while most of the trail could be considered easy, the section through Echo Canyon is very rocky and uneven. The whole thing is intermittently wide and narrow.

THE HIKE

This well-marked trail is a pleasure to hike not only because of the variety of surfaces and views, but also because you'll likely have most of it to yourself as most visitors stick to the popular Summit Trail. But venture out on this longer hike and you'll be well rewarded.

The back side of Enchanted Rock on an early spring day.

Start on the Loop Trail and walk past the picnic tables in the partially shaded grove. The dirt and crushed granite path starts out wide and narrows as it becomes rockier and uneven and winds here and there in and out of partial shade alongside native grasses, wildflowers, live oak, prickly pear and Christmas cactus, and green grasses. You may even spot a few bluebonnets in early spring. And in less than a half a mile you will be treated to impressive views of Enchanted Rock. In fact, for much of the hike the massive batholith will almost always be within view.

This first mile of trail follows Sandy Creek, which is frequently dry if there hasn't been sufficient rain recently. The sound of trickling water will keep you company until you pass the junction for Buzzards Roost camping area when you'll leave the riparian zone and be among large rock structures and formations, including massive layers of sheet rock that the larger stone has shed over the years as it contracts and expands.

At 3.0 miles, turn left onto Echo Canyon Trail. You can continue straight to complete the entire Loop Trail, which you'll have to do if you're hiking with dogs, but Echo Canyon offers a picturesque and interesting change of scenery that's well worth the shortcut, including a view of Moss Lake, where you might see turtles basking.

You'll now be heading toward the back side of Enchanted Rock, so keep an eye out for more

> It's a good idea to make reservations in advance if you plan to visit the park on weekends or holidays. The park is extremely popular and often fills to capacity by morning.

frequent signposts with yellow arrows that will guide you as the narrow trail leads over beds of granite and across shallow creeks as you enter the canyon between Enchanted Rock and Little Enchanted Rock and a popular climbing area.

After you pass the shady climbing area, you'll do a bit of light scrambling over large boulders and granite slopes. Continue to follow the yellow arrows.

Echo Trail dead-ends into the Summit Trail at 3.8 miles. When it does, continue straight across the granite slab and down Summit Trail. If you haven't tackled the summit

The view down the trail from the highest point of the hike.

Little Rock and its reflection in Moss Lake.

of Enchanted Rock yet, you can turn left instead and add an additional 0.6 miles to your hike.

As you reach the bottom, go up a set of wooden stairs that lead to a pavilion with informational signs. Walk straight through it and continue toward the bathroom building, past the upper parking lot, and down the small hill toward the creek below. Cross the creek on the stepping stones, and in just a few more steps up the other side you'll return to the parking lot and trailhead.

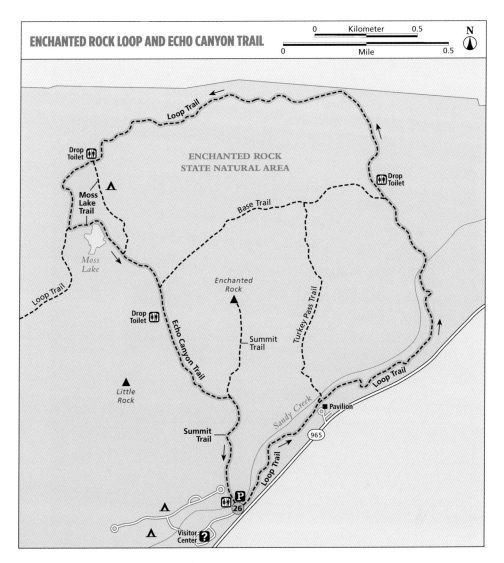

ENCHANTED ROCK LOOP AND ECHO CANYON TRAIL

ENCHANTED ROCK
STATE NATURAL AREA

Drop Toilet

Moss Lake Trail

Moss Lake

Loop Trail

Base Trail

Drop Toilet

Turkey Pass Trail

Drop Toilet

Echo Canyon Trail

Enchanted Rock

Summit Trail

Little Rock

Loop Trail

Sandy Creek

Pavilion

965

Summit Trail

Loop Trail

Visitor Center

P 26

MILES AND DIRECTIONS

0.0 Start from the Loop Trail Trailhead.

0.2 Continue straight past the junction with an unnamed connecting trail.

0.4 Continue to the left past the group pavilion and parking area.

0.4 Continue straight past the junction with Turkey Pass.

1.1 Veer left to continue on the Loop Trail past Buzzards Roost camping area.

1.1 Curve to the left and cross the creek.

1.4 Continue straight at the junction with the unmarked trail.

1.5 Continue straight past Crystal Hill restroom.

2.7 Continue straight past Moss Lake restroom and the junction with the Moss Lake camping area.

A sunny dirt path along the route.

3.0   Turn left onto Echo Canyon Trail.

3.0   Arrive at Moss Lake.

3.1   Turn left onto Echo Canyon Trail.

3.2   Pass the sign for Moss Lake camping area and continue straight.

3.3   Continue straight across an unmarked, narrow dirt path (Base Trail).

3.5   Arrive at a popular climbing area with a drop toilet.

3.6   Veer left following the yellow arrows.

3.6   Curve to the right following the yellow arrows.

3.8   Echo Trail dead-ends into Summit Trail. Continue straight down Summit Trail.

4.1   Arrive at a small pavilion with informational signs. Continue straight toward the bathroom building.

4.2   Arrive back at the trailhead and parking lot.

27 CHARRO RANCH PARK NATURE TRAIL

If you find yourself in Dripping Springs, perhaps staying in nearby cabins or enjoying a locally crafted beverage at one of the area's many breweries, wineries, and distilleries, there's no better place to enjoy a quick and easy but secluded and natural evening stroll than Charro Ranch Park. Limestone, juniper, and live oak abound, and several man-made structures along the mostly flat path invite visitors to slow down, relax, and enjoy all nature has to offer.

Start: Trailhead information sign (visible from the parking lot)
Elevation gain: 1,119 to 1,148 feet
Distance: 1.1-mile lollipop (with option to add on a 1.3-mile loop)
Difficulty: Easy as the trail is flat and wide
Hiking time: 30 minutes
Seasons/schedule: Best in spring, fall, and winter or early morning or late evening in the summer; open from dawn to midnight year-round
Fees and permits: None
Trail contacts: City of Dripping Springs, 22690 W. FM 150 Driftwood, TX 78619; (512) 858-4725; https://www.cityofdrippingsprings.com/our-parks/pages/charro-ranch-park
Canine compatibility: On-leash only

Trail surface: Dirt, mulch, gravel
Land status: City park
Nearest town: Dripping Springs
Other trail users: Hikers only
Maps: USGS Dripping Springs Quadrangle; University of Texas, https://maps.lib.utexas.edu/maps/topo/texas/geopdf_2013/dripping_springs-2012.pdf
Water availability: None
Special considerations: Some of this trail is in full sun and can be very hot in the summer. There is no water available.
Amenities available: Porta-potties, shelter, picnic tables
Maximum grade: 4% for 0.1 miles
Cell service: Throughout

FINDING THE TRAILHEAD

From FM 150, turn onto the gravel drive at the sign for Charro Ranch Park. The short drive will lead you to the gravel parking lot at the trailhead.
GPS: 30.160353, -98.072971

Trail conditions: The trail is almost completely flat, wide, and easy with sections of gravel, grass, and dirt. In a few sections, limestone from below the surface pop up to create rocky sections, but these are brief. Some of the trail is in full sun, but much is in partial shade.

THE HIKE

This unpretentious gem of a park located just a few minutes from the center of Dripping Springs offers the perfect place to escape for a quiet morning or evening stroll. Rarely busy, wide, easy trails wind through juniper and live oak and the trail is flanked by prickly pear cacti and waving grasses, plus wildflowers in the spring.

The 64–acre park is largely maintained by Hays County Master Naturalist volunteers, but the land was originally donated by Lucy Reed Hibberd in 2008 and it was she who developed trails and created area for reflection, including a solstice circle and Walk of

Wildflowers can be spotted in warmer months but especially in the spring.

Peace, both of which can be found on the Nature Trail (or Fox Trail—it's marked with the outline of a fox head).

    Start your hike at the information board to the right of the entrance. You'll see it from the parking lot along with a bird viewing station on the left. Head to the right. You'll immediately pass a small, partially shaded picnic area with tables, then at the junction, turn left to continue on Nature Trail.

A picturesque wooden bridge along the trail.

Shortly, you'll pass through a metal arch and arrive at the Solstice Circle where an informational sign explains the summer and winter solstice, equinox and cardinal directions, plus how the circular stone and cement structure marks the position of the sun in the sky at various times of year.

Continue on the Nature Trail through the arch on the other side of the circle. In a few steps, at the next junction, continue straight to stay on the trail marked with a green P (for parking) and a blue peace sign. This is the beginning of the loop portion of the trail.

Continue to follow the markers with a peace sign and watch for uneven rock underfoot and at 0.4 miles, you'll reach the Peace Circle. Take a break in the shade or meander around the labyrinth-like circle.

Top: The entry arch into the Solstice Circle.
Bottom: The Peace Circle.

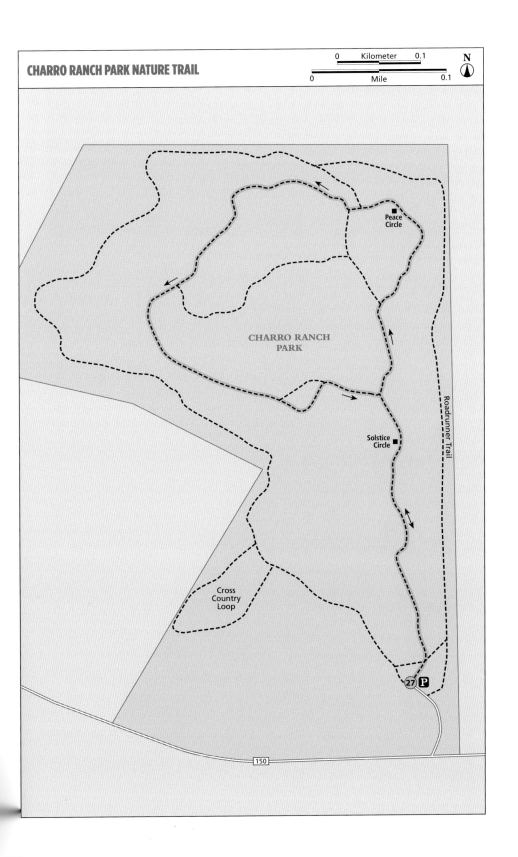

0   Kilometer   0.1

0   Mile   0.1

N

Peace
Circle

CHARRO RANCH
PARK

Roadrunner Trail

Solstice
Circle

Cross
Country
Loop

27 P

150

Picnic tables in the shade.

At the junction just a few feet from the Peace Circle, turn right onto the trail marked with the red fox and continue to follow it as you walk, all the way to a wooden footbridge fringed with wildflowers that pop up in spring and early summer.

The trail runs into the stem of the lollipop at 0.9 miles. Turn right, following the signs with the green P, to retrace your steps from the first 0.2 miles of the hike.

When you return to the trailhead at 1.1 miles, take a break at the shaded observation deck and marvel at the yucca, chaparral berry, and agave plants as you watch for a variety of birds that call the area home.

Want to lengthen your walk by an additional 1.3 miles? Head back to the first junction and take the Cross Country Loop for another easy, sunny stroll and more wide-open views.

MILES AND DIRECTIONS

0.0 Start from the informational sign at the trailhead and head right. Pass picnic tables, and turn left at the junction to take Nature Trail.

0.2 Arrive at the Solstice Circle. Continue straight to the other side.

0.2 Continue straight at the intersection to stay on Nature Trail (marked with a blue peace sign).

0.3 Veer right, following the peace signs.

0.4 Arrive at the Peace Circle.

0.5 At the junction just a few feet from the Peace Circle, turn right onto the trail marked with the red fox.

0.6 At the intersection, continue straight to stay on Nature Trail.

0.8 Cross the wooden bridge.

0.9 Turn right following the signs with the green P to head back to the trailhead parking lot. Retrace your steps from the first 0.2 miles of the trail.

1.1 Arrive back at the trailhead.

Dripping Springs is home to many distilleries and breweries. For a unique Hill Country sip, stop by Desert Door for a sotol cocktail. Nearby, Getaway tiny cabins offer a place for hikers to relax in nature for a few nights.

This frequently sunny ramble is located in a park that owes its popularity to its namesake feature: a deep swimming hole along a creek that leads down to an underwater cave system. But while the caves aren't explorable recreationally, the swimming hole is open to those who want to enjoy a dip on a hot summer day (reservations required) and a series of trails through varied terrain offer a pleasant way to explore the area any time of year.

Start: Jacob's Well Trailhead across the park road from parking lot A and B
Elevation gain: 922 to 1,030 feet
Distance: 1.4-mile circuit
Difficulty: Easy due to mostly flat trails with a few short ups and downs
Hiking time: 45 minutes
Seasons/schedule: Daily year-round, though trails get hot in the summer; swimming reservations are only open May 1–Sept 30. Park open 8 a.m.–6 p.m.
Fees and permits: Park is free to enter, but swimming requires reservations: Hays County residents, children 5–12, seniors, and veterans $5; all other adults $9; under 4 free
Trail contacts: Hays County Parks Department, 1699 Mt. Sharp Rd., Wimberley, TX 78676; (512) 214-4593; https://hayscountytx.com/ departments/hays-county-parks-recreation/jacobs-well-natural-area/#contact
Canine compatibility: No dogs allowed
Trail surface: Dirt, stone
Land status: County Park
Nearest town: Wimberley
Other trail users: Hikers only
Maps: Hays County Map: http://visit wimberley.com/jacobswell/images/ JWNA_map_ks.jpg
Water availability: At Nature Center
Special considerations: Trails are mostly sunny and hot in the summer. Swimming is not permitted Oct 1–Apr 30.
Amenities available: Restrooms, picnic tables, shelter, nature center, water fountains
Maximum grade: 10% for 0.4 miles
Cell service: Throughout

FINDING THE TRAILHEAD

From the park entrance, drive to parking lot A or B. Cross the park road on foot to get to the trailhead on the other side, following signs for Jacob's Well. **GPS:** 30.038602, -98.127253

Trail conditions: The trail starts as a wide, flat, crushed gravel path through prairie but alternates between gravel, dirt, and limestone. Much of the trail is in full sun, making it hot in the summer, but some sections provide partial shade.

THE HIKE

Jacob's Well Natural Area may span 81 acres, but the main attraction at this Hill Country park is the well itself: an artesian spring that stays at a brisk 68°F year-round and also happens to be the second-largest fully submerged cave in Texas. Divers shouldn't get too excited, though—many have perished over the years in the deep, dark recesses of the cavern system that's about 140 feet deep and 4,341 feet long, so diving is no longer permitted.

Jacob's Well features limestone cliffs on one side, perfect for jumping into the water in the summer.

But swimming is permitted in the well that also happens to be the headwaters of Cypress Creek, which flows through popular Blue Hole Regional Park (Hike 29) just down the road.

This hike will lead you to the swimming hole (reservations are required to swim in the summer) and also along a winding path around much of the park.

Walking along a sunny, wide, crushed granite portion of trail.

The trail starts as a large, flat, wide dirt and gravel path through sunny prairie peppered with juniper, povertyweed, Texas persimmon, frostweed, live oak, and even yucca. When you pass the labyrinth on your right, take a pit stop to wander the meditative path, then return to the main path to continue on.

At 0.3 miles, descend the rocky steps that lead down toward the well. At the bottom, turn left for upper access to the well and follow along the low cliff face to the low

Top: A directional sign for Warbler Woodlands.
Bottom left: The creek beyond the underground cave.
Bottom right: A rustic natural staircase along the trail.

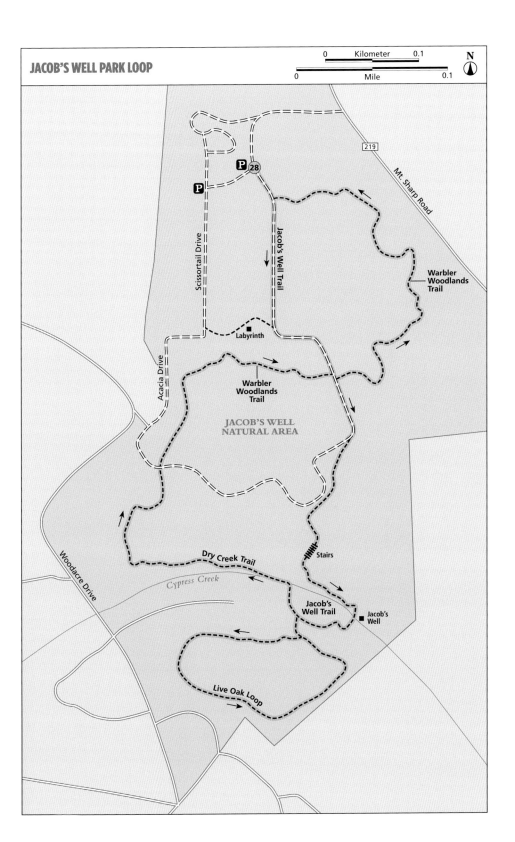

JACOB'S WELL PARK LOOP

0 Kilometer 0.1

0 Mile 0.1

N

219

Mt. Sharp Road

P 28
P

Scissortail Drive

Jacob's Well Trail

Acacia Drive

Labyrinth

Warbler
Woodlands
Trail

Warbler
Woodlands
Trail

JACOB'S WELL
NATURAL AREA

Stairs

Dry Creek Trail

Cypress Creek

Woodacre Drive

Jacob's
Well Trail

Jacob's
Well

Live Oak Loop

overlook. If you have a swimming reservation, jump right in; the cavern below the surface means the water is plenty deep. Or scramble down the rocks and cross the creek on the cement boardwalk to continue on your way.

At the next junction, turn left, away from the signs pointing to parking and the nature center followed by a near immediate right onto Live Oak Loop. This part of the trail offers very little shade, but there are a few benches on which to sit and rest under the branches of pecan and live oak trees.

When you return to the beginning of the Live Oak Loop, continue straight toward the sign for the nature center and parking lot, then turn left, go down a brief set of steps, and turn left again onto Dry Creek Trail. The rocky riparian path features cattails, American sycamore, and tiny white-topped sedge as it leads you between trees and greenery on your left and limestone rock faces on your right.

When you reach the stairs, go up. At the top, a narrow paved path will lead the way to the nature center where you can take a break at shaded picnic tables, fill up your water bottle, or visit the center when it's open.

From here, follow signs for the parking lot and the labyrinth to transition to Warbler Woodlands Trail.

At 1.2 miles, the trail splits and rejoins just a minute or two down the path, but continue on the trail to the right to complete the outside loop of the Warbler Woodlands Trail and end up back at Jacob's Well Trail just a few feet from the trailhead and parking lot.

MILES AND DIRECTIONS

0.0   Start at Jacob's Well Trailhead.

0.1   A sign will point to the labyrinth on your right.

0.2   At the intersection, follow signs for the well, take the trail to the right, then follow the trail to the left to start heading down.

0.3   Steps lead down to the well. At the bottom, turn left for upper access.

0.4   Reach the top of Jacob's Well. Scramble down the rocks onto the cement boardwalk and across the walkway to the other side of the creek. Continue straight, then turn left on Live Oak Loop.

0.6   Continue straight at the unmarked intersection.

0.7   Arrive back at the beginning of Live Oak Loop. Continue straight toward the sign that points to the nature center and parking lot. Turn left onto the dirt and gravel path toward the nature center.

0.8   Turn left onto Dry Creek Trail.

0.9   Turn right and go up the steps. Pass the nature center.

1.0   Continue straight toward the sign for the parking lot and labyrinth.

1.1   The trail curves to the right.

1.2   Cross Jacob's Well Trail and continue on Warbler Woodlands Trail. Continue straight at the intersection.

1.4   Turn right onto Jacob's Well Trail. Arrive back at trailhead and parking lot.

29 BLUE HOLE REGIONAL PARK CYPRESS CREEK NATURE TRAIL

This short and sweet hike may be easy, but it's well worth treading the delightfully shaded, earthen path for the clear creek views, towering cypress trees, and the payoff at both ends of the out-and-back route: food, drinks, and shopping on one end, the lovely and popular Wimberley Blue Hole on the other. Don't forget to make a reservation to take a dip in the summer!

Start: The Cypress Creek Nature Trail Trailhead at Blue Hole Regional Park
Elevation gain: 832 to 863 feet
Distance: 1.2-mile out-and-back
Difficulty: Easy thanks to flat trails and abundant shade
Hiking time: 30 minutes
Seasons/schedule: Year-round
Fees and permits: None
Trail contacts: City of Wimberley Parks and Recreation, 100 Blue Hole Ln., Wimberley, TX 78676; (512) 660-9111; https://www.cityofwimberley.com/157/Parks-Recreation
Canine compatibility: On-leash only
Trail surface: Crushed granite, mulch, dirt
Land status: City park

Nearest town: Wimberley
Other trail users: Hikers only
Maps: City of Wimberley, https://www.cityofwimberley.com/ImageRepository/Document?documentID=549
Water availability: Yes
Special considerations: You cannot swim in the creek, but you can swim in Blue Hole Regional Park for a fee, though advance reservations are required.
Amenities available: Restrooms, picnic tables, shelter
Maximum grade: 15% for less than 0.1 miles
Cell service: Throughout

FINDING THE TRAILHEAD

From the parking lot or street parking along Blue Hole Road, walk to the ticket station at the entrance to Blue Hole. Turn left to go down the crushed gravel path along the side of the parking area. The trail begins after you walk through the metal gate at the end of the parking lot. **GPS:** 30.002486, -98.090717

Trail conditions: While the first short section of the trail is in full sun, it soon enters shaded forest where it remains for the rest of the hike. The trail is often wide enough for two, firm packed dirt, and flat with few trail hazards.

THE HIKE

Stretching from the southwestern edge of Blue Hole Regional Park to just east of Wimberley Square, this trail traverses acres of protected preserve and creekside forest, land that has never been farmed or developed. It's a pristine riparian ecosystem, home to a wide variety of plants and wildlife, including bald cypress trees, frostweed, mustang grape, and mulberry trees, plus birds like belted kingfisher, eastern bluebird, northern cardinal, and more.

It's a shaded waterfront oasis for most of the trail, with a wide-open, sunny section for the first (and last) chunk. And while it may not seem long enough to warrant your attention, the fun that awaits on either end makes it worth the half hour it takes to hike this out-and-back.

Cypress trees line the creek bed.

Park benches at the end of the trail offer a place to sit, relax, and enjoy the scenery.

At one end: downtown Wimberley, complete with shopping, dining, cold drinks, and a wadable section of Cypress Creek behind a local restaurant. At the other end: stunning local swimming hot spot Blue Hole Regional Park where, during summer months, you can make a reservation to take a dip in the cool blue waters of Cypress Creek, fed by nearby Jacob's Well (Hike 19).

From the buildings and ticket station at Blue Hole, take the crushed gravel path to the south end of the parking lot. You'll then pass through a metal gate and over a residential drive to start the trail proper.

As you traverse this sunny section, expect honey mesquite, live oak, juniper, and prairie grasses along the path. At 0.2 miles, pass the junction with the Boy Scout Trail on the left and continue on the Nature Trail. In a few steps, there is a sign with a map of the Nature Trail before the dirt path leads down into shaded creekside forest.

Instead of swimming, which isn't allowed in the protected area, enjoy the views of limestone cliffs on one side of the trail and the creek on the other. Homes dot the landscape here and there on both sides among inland wild oats and Turk's cap that carpet the forest floor in lush greenery. Towering, wide, far-reaching cypress trees line the bank of a trail that is frequently deserted, which offers a pleasant, relaxing, and secluded walk in the woods.

You'll reach the end of the trail at 0.6 miles. A rope across what used to be a path bars entry, but the other trailhead that officially marks the terminus (or the turnaround) is located at the pocket park—complete with playground, picnic tables, and garden pond—up the wheelchair ramp to the left.

Slightly farther past the official end of the trail is a small section of public park, part of which is privately owned by a local restaurant. This area offers several places to sit along the creekside, get in the water, and enjoy the shade. There is even an artful carving of a mermaid in one of the tree stumps along the bank. Access this section by going up to the pocket park, turning right down the main road, then heading back down to the creek from the sidewalk.

Retrace your steps back to the Nature Trail Trailhead and Blue Hole Park.

Top left: The clear creek runs alongside the trail almost the whole way.
Top right: A shady, wooded trail offers a peaceful walking experience.
Bottom: A brief sunny section before the trail leads you into the woods.

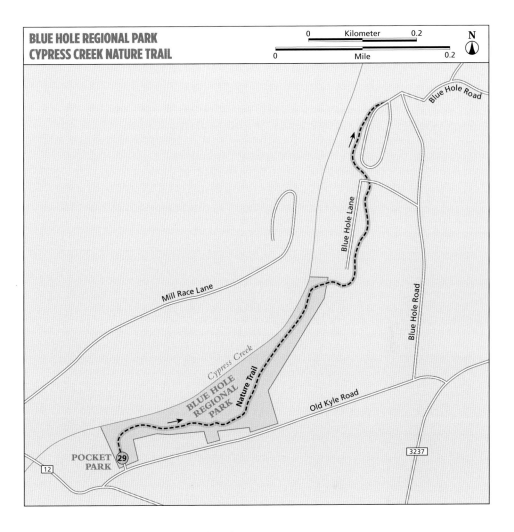

MILES AND DIRECTIONS

0.0 Start from the Blue Hole entrance building and take the crushed gravel path down the length of the parking lot.

0.1 Pass through a metal gate and over a residential drive.

0.2 Pass the junction with Boy Scout Trail. In a few steps, locate a sign with a map of the nature trail.

0.6 Turn left when the trail dead-ends and head up the wheelchair ramp to the pocket park and trailhead. Turn around and retrace your steps.

1.2 Arrive back at the Nature Trail Trailhead and Blue Hole Park.

You can also hike this trail in reverse from the pocket park in Wimberley, an excellent option if you are staying in town and would like to pay a visit to Blue Hole. Travel in either direction and you can enjoy a swim or a bite to eat, a cold beverage, or shopping. If you plan to swim in Blue Hole, reservations are required.

30 PURGATORY CREEK NATURAL AREA LOOP

Ashe juniper, live oak, Texas persimmon, and more Hill Country flora abound on this mostly shaded path within San Marcos city limits. The rocky trail makes for a slightly technical but extremely picturesque hike among juniper forest, open meadows, and live oak branches that hang low over the trail, their tiny leaves sent cascading down from the treetops above like yellow confetti with the slightest breeze. Limestone features, abundant wildlife, and a handful of viewpoints make this hike an exceedingly pleasant diversion.

Start: The Upper Purgatory Trailhead
Elevation gain: 600 to 751 feet
Distance: 8.1-mile double loop
Difficulty: Moderate due to length and regular elevation change
Hiking time: 4 hours
Seasons/schedule: Year-round
Fees and permits: None
Trail contacts: San Marcos Parks and Recreation, 630 E Hopkins St., San Marcos, TX 78666; (512) 393-8400; https://www.sanmarcostx.gov/Facilities/Facility/Details/Purgatory-Creek-Natural-Area-52
Canine compatibility: On-leash only
Trail surface: Dirt, rock
Land status: City park
Nearest town: San Marcos

Other trail users: Mountain bikes
Maps: San Marcos Greenbelt Alliance; https://smgreenbelt.org/wp-content/uploads/2020/09/Purgatory-8.5x11-update-9.9.2020.pdf
Water availability: None
Special considerations: There is no water available at the trailhead, so plan accordingly. Note that golden-cheeked warbler nesting season is from Mar 1 to May 31, and if hiking during this time you will have to take an alternate route of similar distance.
Amenities available: Restrooms
Maximum grade: 7% for 0.3 miles
Cell service: Throughout

FINDING THE TRAILHEAD

From TX 12, turn onto Craddock Avenue toward a neighborhood development. Take the first right onto a road that will quickly become a gravel drive. Continue for 0.5 miles until you reach the trailhead parking lot. **GPS:** 29.883706, -97.977716

Trail conditions: The trails in this green space offer a wide variety of surfaces and views, from dirt and gravel paths to rocky single track. The whole trail is mostly shaded, making for a pleasant hike just about any time of year.

THE HIKE

This long, meandering collection of looping trails offers a picturesque, and often quiet, escape to nature in a lovely green space, most of which feels much farther removed from its urban location than it is. While the lower trailhead is more popular and often filled with cars on weekends, the upper trailhead and loop is slightly less crowded. As a bonus, the section of Dante Trail that connects the two is frequently devoid of any people at all.

That said, if you don't want to tackle the whole 8.1 miles, you can cut it down to 3.2 by just completing the upper loop (Dante, Paraiso, and Styx). However, meadows, forest,

A trail marker on an Ashe juniper along the trail.

overlooks, and abundant wildlife, including deer and birds, make the trek more than worth the effort.

Purgatory Creek, part of Edwards Aquifer, flows through the park, carving creek beds and grottoes along the way, though the creek is frequently dry during seasons of low rainfall.

In forested sections, the dirt path is often strewn with rocks, mostly limestone, and covered in a carpet of live oak leaves. In meadows, tall grasses and wildflowers abound and prickly pear cactus pepper the sides of the trail. Much of the hike is flat or set at gradual angles, but a few sections of ups and downs provide enough variety to get your heart pumping.

At the trailhead, two trails branch off: the ADA-accessible Styx Trail and Dante Trail, which connects to the lower trailhead. Take the Dante Trail, a narrow crushed-gravel path to the right of the informational signs that leads into the woods.

In the first mile, keep an eye out for photo ops of unique live oak trees, including a bearded oak and one that looks like a rhino, and at 1.5 miles, take the trail to the right when it splits for a brief connector trail to a nice view of the surrounding hills.

As you slowly descend, cacti begin to give way to more plant life like giant ragweed, native grasses, and the occasional yucca. You may spot mealy blue sage in meadows, silver-leaf nightshade, thistles, and almost certainly deer. Sections of the trail, particularly once you have descended into the valley, follow along the creek bed below high limestone walls speckled with ferns and cacti.

Because this is a semi urban trail, several sections involve walking within sight of houses built up on high hills, crossing under power lines and bridges, and occasional road noises from the highway nearby. But overall it is a quiet and natural trail.

A rocky overlook.

On your return trip, when you reach the intersection with Paraiso and Dante, turn left to take Paraiso Trail unless you're visiting during golden-cheeked warbler nesting season from March 1 through May 31, when that trail is closed. If signs are posted, continue on Dante instead.

When you reach Styx Trail, take the ADA-accessible gravel path, some of which is through a meadow in full sun. There are a few partially shaded sections, but the Styx Trail is wide, mostly flat, and makes for a quick but still picturesque route back to the trailhead surrounded by live oak and Ashe juniper plus plenty of greenery and several benches in the shade that offer hikers a place to stop and rest.

MILES AND DIRECTIONS

0.0 Start from the Upper Purgatory Trailhead and head right onto Dante Trail.

0.4 Continue on Dante.

The trail winding down into the valley.

0.5	Continue straight on Dante.
1.2	Continue straight on Dante.
1.5	Take the trail to the right for a viewpoint then meet back up with the main trail and continue right in a few steps.
1.8	Veer left to continue on Dante.
2.3	At the intersection with Dante and Beatrice, continue straight.
2.8	Veer left to continue on Dante.
3.0	Turn left to stay on Dante.
3.4	Turn left to stay on Dante.
3.5	Veer right to continue on Dante under the bridge.
3.6	Turn right to continue on Dante.
3.7	At the multi-trail intersection, take Nimrod Trail.
3.9	Turn right to stay on Nimrod Trail when the trail splits in a few more steps. Go straight across a gravel path that leads to the top of the dam. Turn left onto Beatrice Trail.
4.0	Continue straight to stay on Beatrice.
4.1	Continue straight to continue on Beatrice.
4.2	Turn left to stay on Beatrice.
4.3	At the intersection, continue straight to stay on Beatrice.

PURGATORY CREEK NATURAL AREA LOOP

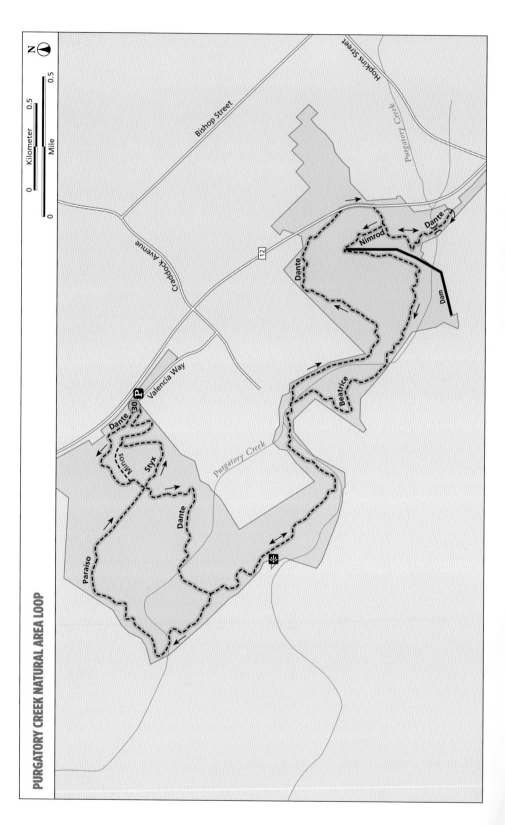

A rocky path in the sun.

4.4 At the intersection, continue straight to stay on Beatrice.

5.2 At the intersection, turn left to return to Dante.

5.7 Veer right to stay on Dante.

5.9 Keep right at the fork to continue on Dante.

6.2 Turn left to take Paraiso Trail. (During golden-cheeked warbler nesting season, March 1 through May 31, continue on Dante instead.)

6.9 Paraiso curves left, Minotaur Canyon viewpoint to the right.

7.3 Continue straight onto Styx Trail.

7.4 At the intersection, continue straight onto Styx.

7.8 Turn right to stay on Styx as it curves sharply to the right.

8.1 Arrive back at the trailhead.

31 SPRING LAKE PRESERVE: ROADRUNNER AND GREY FOX LOOP

Winding trails, abundant greenery, excellent birding, and terrain that varies from wide paths to narrow and ever-changing single track make you forget this is an urban hike in city-owned and -maintained green space. While a good portion of this trail is largely flat, there are several sections of small, rolling hills, and a few longer, rocky slopes that make for delightfully varied terrain.

Start: Begin at the Lime Kiln Trailhead and take the trail to the right after you pass the informational sign
Elevation gain: 591 to 743 feet
Distance: 3.5-mile loop
Difficulty: Moderate due to rocky trail and several ups and downs
Hiking time: 2 hours
Seasons/schedule: Summer, fall, winter
Fees and permits: None
Trail contacts: San Marcos Parks and Recreation, 630 E Hopkins St., San Marcos, TX 78666; (512) 393-8400; http://www.sanmarcostx.gov
Canine compatibility: On-leash only
Trail surface: Dirt, rock
Land status: City park

Nearest town: San Marcos
Other trail users: Mountain bikers
Maps: San Marcos Greenbelt Alliance; https://smgreenbelt.org/new-map-spring-lake-preserve/, https://www.sanmarcostx.gov/DocumentCenter/View/15986/Spring-Lake-Natural-Area-Map-PDF
Water availability: None
Special considerations: Part of the trail is closed from March 31 to May 31 for golden-cheeked warbler nesting season, so always adhere to posted restrictions and find an alternate route during these 3 months of the year.
Amenities available: Restrooms
Maximum grade: 8% for 0.4 miles
Cell service: Throughout

FINDING THE TRAILHEAD

Park at the Lime Kiln Road parking lot. Trailhead off of Lime Kiln Road. The trailhead is located in the corner of the lot. **GPS:** 29.903578, -97.929750

Trail conditions: This natural urban park features a variety of interconnected trails, most of which are well-marked and blazed with color-coded metal markers. There is some elevation gain and loss on trails that are intermittently flat gravel paths and rocky dirt tracks, but much of the hike is in at least partial shade.

THE HIKE

Spring Lake Natural Area offers 251 acres of undeveloped parkland right in the heart of San Marcos. Plenty of interconnected trails offer the option to wander for hours, but the northern trails in particular are an exceedingly pleasant place to explore.

The park is located just above the headwaters of the San Marcos River and approximately half of the property is in the Edwards Aquifer recharge zone within the Edwards

> Maps at the trailhead feature a QR code that lets you scan and load an interactive map of the park so you can track your location.

A live oak draped with Spanish moss.

Plateau. Practically speaking, that means in seasons of sufficient rainfall, Skink Creek and its surrounding springs and tributaries offer several places to sit, relax, and cool off. That said, don't be surprised if creek beds are dry; much of the year, this area doesn't receive enough precipitation to fill swimming holes.

But whether or not water is flowing, there's plenty to delight your senses, including meadows and woodlands, wildflowers in the spring, majestic live oaks draped with Spanish moss, and deer sightings are practically guaranteed.

The path, which is often covered with yellow and brown live oak leaves shed by the gnarly, twisted arms of the trees above, is frequently narrow and winding with many rocky sections, but it is very pleasant and green in places, especially where wild inland oats grow in abundance. Some sections that aren't rock-strewn can be muddy after a rain, and the parks department recommends hikers avoid the area when it is.

A small pond along the trail.

Anytime you visit, start on Blue Heron Trail, often labeled simply as "Heron." You'll only be on it for a few moments before turning right onto Centipede Trail, which is pleasantly wooded, mostly shaded, and you'll be surrounded by plenty of Ashe juniper and Texas persimmon.

From there you will transition to several other trails: Porcupine, Roadrunner, Grey Fox, Blue Stem, Buckeye Trail, and finally Heron once more.

As you wander down the trail, keep an eye out for prickly pear cactus, honey mesquite, wildflowers in the spring, agarita, even a stray palmetto. From time to time, you'll even

An overlook from the path.

be treated to sweepings views of the hills and farmland that lay beyond the boundaries of the park.

At 1.4 miles, Roadrunner Loop marks the beginning of the section of trail (including Grey Fox) that's closed from March 31 to May 31 for golden-cheeked warbler nesting season, so always adhere to posted restrictions and find an alternate route during these three months of the year.

At 3.4 miles, just after you turn onto Heron Trail, you'll arrive at a wooden platform with a bench that overlooks a small pond. Take a moment to enjoy the view, then

SPRING LAKE PRESERVE: ROADRUNNER AND GREY FOX LOOP

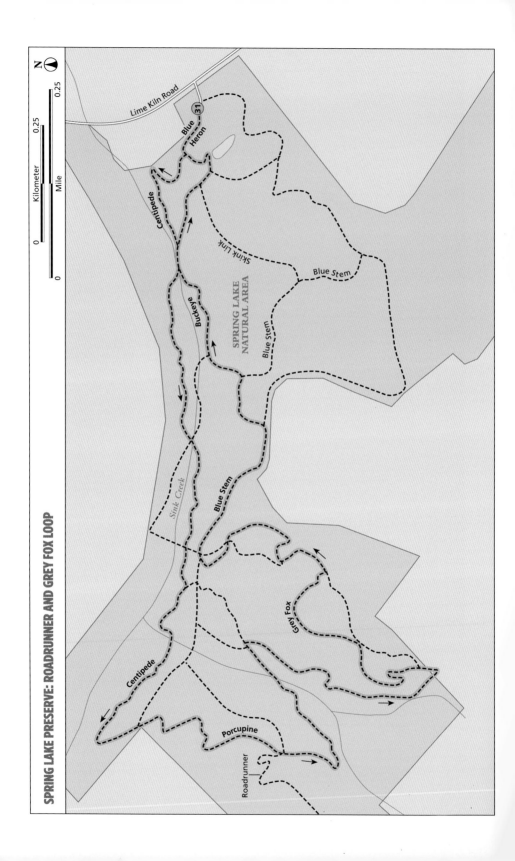

continue on the trail as it curves away from the pond and continue straight ahead down the wide, rocky path back to the trailhead.

MILES AND DIRECTIONS

0.0 Start from Lime Kiln Trailhead and take Blue Heron Trail to the right.

0.1 Turn right at the junction onto Centipede Trail.

0.3 Veer right at the intersection where Centipede and Buckeye Trails briefly overlap. Veer right at the fork to continue on Centipede Trail.

0.7 Continue right to stay on Centipede. At the next junction, continue straight onto Centipede.

0.8 Pass a creek and small waterfall.

0.9 Cross over the top of the falls.

1.1 Veer right to continue on Porcupine Trail at the intersection of Centipede, Porcupine, and Blue Stem.

1.2 Continue straight through an unmarked intersection.

Gnarled branches and rocky trails.

1.4 Take the trail on the left to continue onto Roadrunner (closed from March 31 to May 31).

1.5 Continue right at another unmarked connector trail intersection to stay on Roadrunner.

1.6 Cross a creek bed.

1.7 Turn right onto Grey Fox Trail.

2.0 Turn left onto the rocky path under the power lines to continue on Gray Fox. Take a sharp left onto Grey Fox Trail at the top of the hill.

2.3 Turn right to stay on Grey Fox toward Ironweed Holler.

2.7 Continue straight across the utility path. Turn right onto Blue Stem Trail.

3.0 Turn left onto Buckeye Trail.

3.2 Veer right to stay on Buckeye Trail. Continue right on Buckeye Trail.

3.3 Continue straight at the intersection with Skink Link to continue on Buckeye Trail.

3.4 Veer left onto Blue Heron Trail. Arrive at the pond. Continue straight to stay on Blue Heron.

3.5 Arrive back at the trailhead.

32 GUADALUPE RIVER STATE PARK BALD CYPRESS TRAIL

Beautiful scenery, a variety of plant life, and flowing water make this easy wander a must-do in Hill Country whether you're enjoying fall foliage or you brought your tube to relax and float as you soak up the summer sun. The hike can be extended with a shallow river crossing, but you may find that simply taking your time to sit and enjoy the views along the way are more than enough to satisfy as you appreciate the imposing limestone cliffs across the chattering river.

Start: Bald Cypress Trailhead
Elevation gain: 1,078 to 1,214 feet
Distance: 1.2-mile out-and-back
Difficulty: Easy due to minimal elevation gain, wide trails, and even trail surface
Hiking time: 30 minutes
Seasons/schedule: Year-round, daily 8 a.m.–10 p.m.
Fees and permits: Day-use fee 13+ $7, 12 and under free
Trail contacts: Guadalupe River State Park, 3350 Park Rd. 31, Spring Branch, TX 78070; (830) 438-2656; https://tpwd.texas.gov/state-parks/guadalupe-river
Canine compatibility: On-leash only

Trail surface: Gravel, dirt, asphalt
Land status: Texas Parks and Wildlife Department
Nearest town: Bulverde
Other trail users: Hikers only
Maps: TPWD, https://tpwd.texas.gov/publications/pwdpubs/media/park_maps/pwd_mp_p4505_0040j.pdf
Water availability: Yes, at restrooms
Special considerations: This trail is often busy on weekends during summer months, when the river is a popular swimming spot.
Amenities available: Restrooms, picnic tables, shelter, charcoal grills
Maximum grade: 5% for 0.1 miles
Cell service: Throughout

FINDING THE TRAILHEAD

From the park entrance, drive down the park road to the large parking lot at the very end of the road near the Discovery Center. The trailhead is at the far end of the lot at a metal gate where there's a wide gravel path with an informational sign featuring a map of park trails. **GPS:** 29.875043, -98.485945

Trail conditions: The trail begins as a wide gravel path, then is intermittently packed dirt, gravel, and occasionally rough asphalt. It is generally wide and partially shaded, mostly level with some gradual and brief inclines and declines. There are plenty of access points to the river.

THE HIKE

This easy stroll along the Guadalupe River is one of the most popular in the park for a reason: Not only are there abundant photo ops of limestone cliffs, rocky rapids, and majestic cypress trees, but in the summer this section of river is extremely popular with swimmers trying to escape the Texas heat, and in the late fall, the trees turn a beautiful dusky orange-red, proving that Central Texas enjoys fall foliage, too.

The trail is also a short, sweet, and easy one and offers plenty of places to sit and rest in the shade in the summer or enjoy a picnic at one of the many tables along the way. But the plant and animal life and stunning scenery are what make it a must-see.

Limestone cliffs and cypress trees flank the Guadalupe River, which runs alongside the trail.

For starters, in front of the whimsical Discovery Center on the edge of the trailhead parking lot is an official monarch way station where fans of pollinators can spot a myriad of fluttering creatures, especially during twice-yearly migration.

Then, as you hike, cowpen daisies and other wildflowers line the trail alongside a pecan tree or two. Wingleaf soapberry turns bright gold in the fall, sugar hackberry lends additional foliage and the occasional dwarf palmetto can be spotted, too. Box elder trees provide shade, and in the winter, after freezing temperatures, frostweed stems expel water that freezes into fascinating white ribbon-like shapes.

As your wander down the trail, the riverbank on your left, watch for swallows darting to and away from their nests in the dramatic, jagged cliffs on the other side. Continue the straight, uncomplicated route until you reach the end of the trail. It's unmarked, but you'll know you've arrived by the presence of rocky rapids and a trail that devolves into a jumble of cypress roots.

This is a beautiful spot to enjoy the view, take a dip, or just relax and listen to the rush of water over the rocks. You can also cross the river at this point if you want to hike in the Bauer Unit on the other side. A crossing will require you to get your feet wet except perhaps during times of drought when the water may be low enough for you to rock-hop all the way across.

Once you reach the end of the trail, turn around and retrace your steps back toward the trailhead. Alternatively, at 0.8 miles, there is a dirt path that leads down to a narrow trail and the rocky riverbank. As long as the water isn't abnormally high, you can walk along a narrow dirt path or the river for more up-close waterfront views.

There are also different varieties of native plant life nearer the water than you'll find on many other trails in Hill Country, such as upright prairie coneflower, rough cocklebur,

The crystal clear Guadalupe River surrounded by colorful cypress trees.

The roots of a mature cypress tree near the river.

Shallow rapids near
the end of the trail.

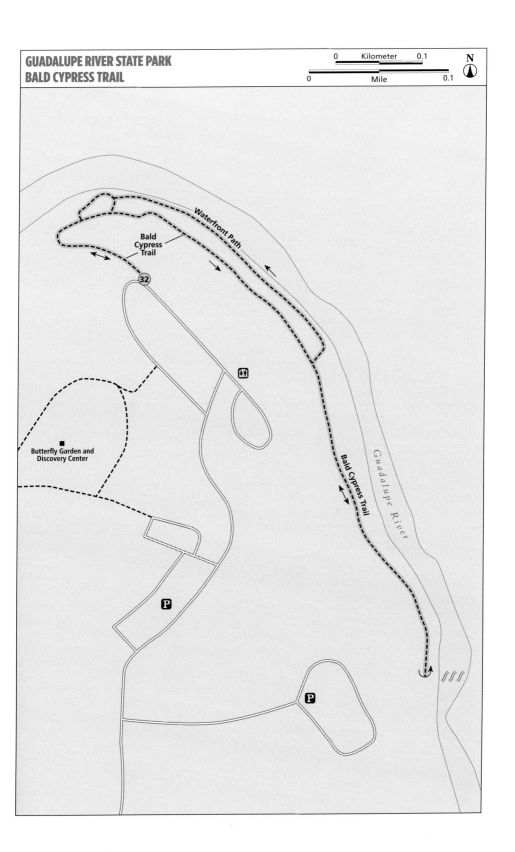

0   Kilometer   0.1

0   Mile   0.1

N

Waterfront Path

Bald
Cypress
Trail

32

Butterfly Garden and
Discovery Center

Bald Cypress Trail

Guadalupe River

P

P

Colorful cypress trees separate the river from the rooty trail in the fall.

Santa Maria feverfew, castor beans, fuzzy-leafed great mullein, and more. So take your time and enjoy the diversity before you head back up to the trailhead.

> Camping is available at the park.

MILES AND DIRECTIONS

0.0 Start from the Bald Cypress Trailhead.

0.3 Continue straight past an asphalt path that leads back up to the bathrooms and parking lot.

0.5 Continue straight past the trail on your right that leads up to another parking lot.

0.6 Reach the end of the trail, turn around, and retrace your steps.

0.8 For a slight variation, veer right down the dirt path that leads toward the river to a narrow dirt trail along the riverbank.

1.1 If you were walking along the riverbed, head back up to the main trail where you will meet the asphalt path and loop back up to the parking lot.

1.2 Arrive back at the trailhead and parking lot.

33 GUADALUPE RIVER STATE PARK CURRY CREEK OVERLOOK

This well-marked trail in the less-crowded unit of Guadalupe River State Park will lead you through sunny, open grassland, wind through partially shaded cedar brakes, and roll through leafy deciduous forest. In the spring, bring your binoculars if you plan to try and spot the endangered golden-cheeked warbler, and in the fall, enjoy the showy color-changing leaves. The Bauer Unit is separated from the main park areas via the Guadalupe River, so you'll have to drive 25 minutes to get there. Just don't forget to pay your entrance fee either at park headquarters or at the self-pay station at the trailhead.

Start: Bamberger Trailhead
Elevation gain: 1,078 to 1,214 feet
Distance: 3.9-mile loop
Difficulty: Easy to moderate due to minimal elevation gain and partial shade but some uneven trail surfaces
Hiking time: 2 hours
Seasons/schedule: Year-round, daily 8 a.m.–10 p.m.
Fees and permits: Day-use fee 13+ $7, 12 and under free
Trail contacts: Guadalupe River State Park, 3350 Park Rd. 31, Spring Branch, TX 78070; (830) 438-2656; https://tpwd.texas.gov/state-parks/guadalupe-river
Canine compatibility: On-leash only
Trail surface: Gravel, dirt

Land status: Texas Parks and Wildlife Department
Nearest town: Spring Branch
Other trail users: Mountain bikes
Maps: TPWD, https://tpwd.texas.gov/publications/pwdpubs/media/park_maps/pwd_mp_p4505_0040j.pdf
Water availability: No
Special considerations: You will find no water, trash cans, or bathrooms at this trailhead, and it is located 14 miles from the main park entrance and visitor center. You still need a day-use pass, which you can get at the visitor center or via a self-pay station at the trailhead.
Amenities available: Bench
Maximum grade: 5% for 0.4 miles
Cell service: Throughout

FINDING THE TRAILHEAD

From the park entrance, turn right on TX 46, right on FM 3351, right on Edge Falls Road and right on Acker Road toward the sign for Guadalupe River State Park Bauer Unit. Down Acker Road 2.2 miles, a large wooden arch and metal gate on a gravel park road signal the unit entrance. Open the gate to get through and close it behind you. The large gravel parking lot is on the right just down the gravel road. The main trailhead is located by another gate a few steps farther down the gravel road past the lot. An informational sign, self-pay station, and maps are available. **GPS:** 29.88522, -98.49606

Trail conditions: Intermittently partially shaded and in full sun. Portions of the trail are flat and wide while others are winding and rocky. Elevation change is gradual.

THE HIKE

If it's quiet and secluded trails you're after, drive away from the main entrance of Guadalupe River State Park and head to the Bauer Unit. Because while the more popular area of the park offers ample reasons to stay and play, it's also quite a bit busier, especially

Top: A rocky section of trail among abundant juniper.
Bottom: A few sections of the trail are wide, flat, and sunny and lead hikers through open prairie.

Narrow, rocky trails lead up and around the overlook.

Stands of Ashe juniper frequently offer at least partial shade.

GUADALUPE RIVER STATE PARK CURRY CREEK OVERLOOK

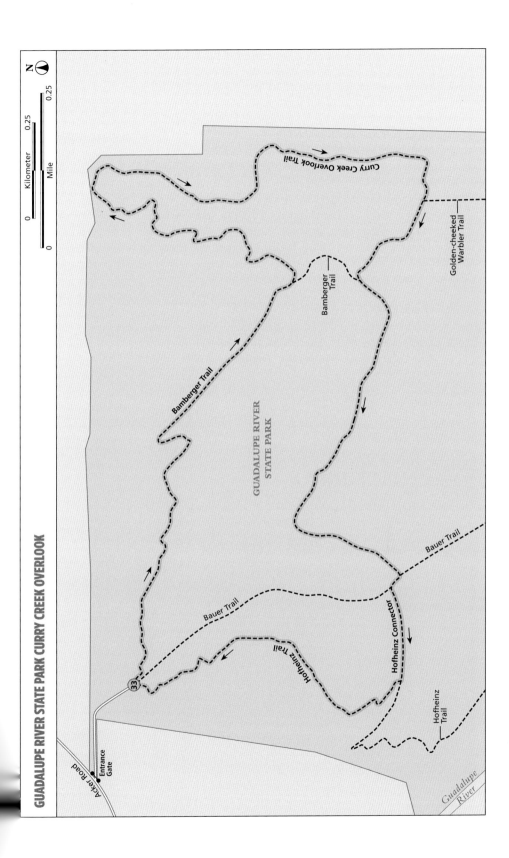

on warm weekends. In the Bauer Unit, on the other hand, you are much more likely to have the trails entirely to yourself. And between overlooks, fall foliage, open prairie, and wildlife, it offers a more than satisfying hike. You can easily tack on a few extra miles or cut your hike short thanks to additional loops.

You'll start in partially shaded Ashe juniper brake where you'll be surrounded by live oak trees and American holly growing in the rocky soil. As you transition to open grassland, Texas mountain laurel, juniper, persimmon and prickly pear cactus sprout in sunny sections and the trail is wide, open, and sunny. Throughout your hike you will move between partially shaded woods and sunny prairies time and time again.

The Curry Creek Overlook Trail is especially picturesque with its narrow, winding, rocky trail and abundance of Buckleys oak, cedar elm, and Texas ash trees that turn gold and orange in November. Here, too, live oaks and juniper are draped with Spanish moss, and you may even spot some color-changing cypress trees along the creek below the ridge trail that's strewn with limestone and frequently edged with piles of pockmarked rock. Geology enthusiasts are sure to enjoy the spring seep and other karst features along the way.

At several junctions after Curry Creek Overlook Trail, you also have the option to extend your hike by turning left on Golden-cheeked Warbler and/or Bauer and Hofheinz Trail. But stay on this mapped loop and you'll likely spot birds, including the golden-cheeked warbler in the spring and summer, deer, and maybe an armadillo or two if you're lucky.

At 3.9 miles you'll reach an unmarked trail junction where the trail curves to the left and you will spot the benches at the main trailhead just up ahead. Arrive back at the parking lot via the dirt path and make sure to close the gate behind you when you drive back onto Acker Road.

MILES AND DIRECTIONS

0.0 Start from the main trailhead, Bamberger Trailhead, and informational sign. Go through the gate and walk a few feet on the wide gravel service road to turn left on Bamberger Trail just ahead.

0.5 Continue on Bamberger Trail as it curves to the right.

0.9 Turn left onto Curry Creek Overlook Trail.

2.2 Turn right onto Golden-cheeked Warbler Trail.

2.4 Turn left to return to Bamberger Trail.

3.1 Turn right onto Bauer Trail.

3.1 Turn left following signs for Hofheinz Connector Trail.

3.3 Turn right onto Hofheinz Trail.

3.9 Continue straight at the unmarked trail junction. The trail curves to the left and you will see the benches at the trailhead just up ahead.

3.9 Arrive back at trailhead.

34 CAVE WITHOUT A NAME RIM LOOP TRAIL

Located on 170 acres of privately owned land, the hiking trails here may not be the main attraction, but they're no less worth a visit. Indeed, most people who find themselves at Cave Without a Name are there for the massive underground cave system for which you can purchase tickets to tour. It's part of the Texas Cave Trail and shouldn't be missed, but whether you pay to get subterranean or not, you're very likely to have the whole trail system to yourself. And that means you can take your time wandering the shady paths, navigating the rocky ups and downs, and enjoying the abundant native flora.

Start: At Cave Without a Name Trailhead; two stone pylons mark the beginning of the grassy dirt path lined with stones
Elevation gain: 1,188 to 1,253 feet
Distance: 1.3-mile loop
Difficulty: Easy due to mostly shaded trail and limited elevation change but with some rocky sections
Hiking time: 45 minutes
Seasons/schedule: Year-round, Labor Day–Memorial Day 10 a.m.–5 p.m., Memorial Day–Labor Day 9 a.m.–6 p.m., closed Thanksgiving and Christmas
Fees and permits: None to use the trails, cave tours are in addition
Trail contacts: Cave Without a Name, 325 Kreutzberg Rd., Boerne, TX 78006; (830) 537-4212; https://www.cavewithoutaname.com

Canine compatibility: On-leash only
Trail surface: Packed dirt and rock
Land status: Privately owned
Nearest town: Boerne
Other trail users: Hikers only
Maps: https://www.cavewithouta name.com/sites/default/files/trail -map.pdf (map may out of date), USGS Kendalia Quadrangle https://maps.lib.utexas.edu/maps/topo/texas/geopdf_2013/kendalia-2013.pdf (trails are not marked)
Water availability: Yes
Special considerations: If you're not camping on-site, you'll have to vacate the premises by closing time.
Amenities available: Restrooms, picnic area, labyrinth, campground
Maximum grade: 8% for 0.1 miles
Cell service: Cell service throughout

FINDING THE TRAILHEAD

From Kreutzberg Road, turn onto the drive at the signposted gate for Cave Without a Name and continue 1 mile to the parking lot. The trailhead is located behind the visitor center building. **GPS:** 29.88623, -98.61758

Trail conditions: The trail is mostly shaded throughout with several overlooks and quick exit points. It's a mostly dirt path with several rocky, uneven sections and brief, only occasionally steep, ups and downs.

In addition to short hikes, this privately owned property hosts events, offers a primitive campground, and offers ticketed tours of the cave system multiple times a day. Stay a while to explore the property and learn about the natural underground wonder. Make reservations in advance to guarantee a spot on a tour.

A wooden footbridge crosses over a dry creek bed in the woods.

THE HIKE

This compact trail system outside of Boerne, Texas, may not be as well advertised or trodden as many others in the area, but that doesn't mean it's less well developed. On the contrary, paths are clear and well-marked, color-coded signs are peppered along the trail, and despite the fact that the trail is not the main attraction at the destination, it's both free and inviting.

Sure, most visitors are there to tour the cave for which the attraction is named (or not named?), but those just wishing to wander the wooded paths are welcome. Although, while you're there, you might as well buy a ticket to get a 60-minute tour of the

The often winding trail is frequently marked with colored paint on the rocks alongside the path.

Top: Ash and oak trees offer welcome shade along most of the trail (and a soft scatter of leaves in the fall).
Bottom: The entrance to the main Cave Without a Name trail system.

CAVE WITHOUT A NAME RIM LOOP TRAIL

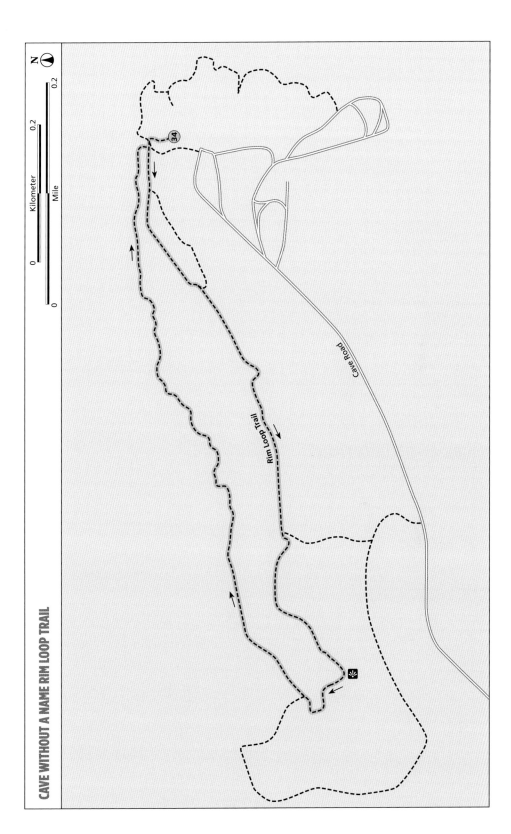

underground marvel. You can even book a primitive campsite on the property if you're looking for a place to spend the night.

As you begin your hike, you'll reach the first junction marked with a color-coded map depicting the trails. There are a handful to choose from, but the Rim Trail is the longest and the only loop. Turn left following signs for Rim Trail, which will be marked by red and blue blazes painted on the stones on the ground.

Then look around you. Right away you'll spot live oak, juniper, Texas persimmon, prickly pear cactus plus Buckley's oak and cedar elm, both of which turn a lovely gold-orange in the fall. The entire trail is mostly shaded thanks to an abundance of foliage overhead, a welcome sight on hot summer days.

When you reach the junction with the loop proper, you can travel in either direction, but turn left onto Rim Trail, which will be marked with red blazes painted on the rock. You'll begin to descend a rocky dirt path. In fact, plan to spend the next mile going up and down short but rocky inclines and declines. On the upside, the trail is easy to follow thanks to frequent blazes on trees and rocks.

As you hike, you'll find a handful of overlooks peppered along the trail. When you do, stop and scan the valley for all the different trees and spot cars driving the winding country roads in the distance.

At 0.2 miles, at the junction with Loop Trail and Rim Trail, veer right to continue on Rim Trail, which will now be marked with blue blazes and surrounded by Mexican buckeye and shin oak. Look for the signs identifying various trees along the way.

By 1.3 miles you'll return to the first trail junction. You'll see red and blue blazes painted on the rocks again and the painted map to your left. Turn left toward it and then immediately right to continue back to the trailhead just a few steps away.

MILES AND DIRECTIONS

0.0 Start from the main trailhead behind the visitor center and gift shop. In a few steps, arrive at the first junction with a color-coded trail map. Turn left following signs for Rim Trail, marked by red and blue blazes.

0.1 At the junction with Rim Loop, turn right onto Rim Loop Trail.

0.2 Veer right at the junction to continue on Rim Trail.

0.4 Pass a side trail for the shortcut exit. Continue straight to stay on Rim Trail. Another color-coded map will identify your location.

0.6 Arrive at an overlook.

1.3 Arrive back at the first junction. Turn left toward the map and then immediately right to continue back to the trailhead. Keep right to continue toward the trailhead. Arrive back at the trailhead.

35 GOVERNMENT CANYON STATE NATURAL AREA JOE JOHNSTON ROUTE

Take an easy, sunny stroll to see fossilized dinosaur tracks embedded in a dry creek bed on this extended, mostly level hike, then wander up to the overlook to gaze down on the prehistoric footprints below and the acres of park beyond. The path is often wide, perfect for wandering and chatting with companions, which makes for a leisurely ramble. Just don't forget to bring enough water as much of the trail is in full sun.

Start: The Backcountry Trailhead
Elevation gain: 1,020 to 1,191 feet
Distance: 6.3-mile lollipop
Difficulty: Easy due to mostly level terrain and gradual inclines
Hiking time: 3 hours
Seasons/schedule: Year-round, Fri–Mon 7 a.m.–10 p.m., closed Tues–Thurs
Fees and permits: Day-use fee 13+ $6, children 12 and under free
Trail contacts: Government Canyon State Natural Area, 12861 Galm Rd., San Antonio, TX 78254; (210) 688-9055; https://tpwd.texas.gov/state-parks/government-canyon
Canine compatibility: No pets allowed
Trail surface: Gravel, dirt, rock

Land status: Texas Parks and Wildlife Department
Nearest town: San Antonio
Other trail users: Mountain bikers (Joe Johnston Route only)
Maps: Texas Parks and Wildlife Department Trail Map, https://tpwd.texas.gov/publications/pwdpubs/media/park_maps/pwd_mp_p4505_0165e.pdf
Water availability: Yes, at visitor center
Special considerations: This exposed trail can be hot in summer. Bring plenty of water.
Amenities available: Restrooms, benches, shelter located at visitor center
Maximum grade: 5% for 0.4 miles
Cell service: Cell service throughout

FINDING THE TRAILHEAD

From the visitor center, walk alongside the building down the cement walkway toward the asphalt trail. Cross the bridge on the sidewalk to get to the Backcountry Trailhead, which is 0.1 miles from the visitor center. Signage will guide the way. **GPS:** 29.550056, -98.762597

Trail conditions: Most of Joe Johnston Route is wide and level, mostly dirt and gravel with little shade. The Overlook Trail is slightly more difficult and narrow with some shade.

THE HIKE

Government Canyon is a surprisingly wild and picturesque place to hike given that it's so close to San Antonio. Within city limits, it offers a beautiful and scientifically relevant getaway from the busy city streets, namely because of the dinosaur tracks found here, which are viewable along this trail. These tracks make the park popular with not only locals on weekends and holidays, but also school groups and scientists.

Dinosaur tracks beneath limestone cliffs.

Note that this natural area is only open Friday to Monday. The park is used for research Tuesday to Thursday. Many trails also close after heavy rains, so check with the park about trail conditions before you arrive. Reservations are recommended on weekends.

Spanish moss draped over live oaks on a shady section of trail.

The tracks include sauropod and theropod prints, a result of dinosaurs that lived in this area during the Cretaceous period. In fact, the reason the natural area is closed Tuesday through Thursday every week is to offer biologists and other scientists a quiet place to conduct research.

But dinosaur tracks (which are easily viewable but roped off to preserve their integrity) aren't the only attraction: The sculpted limestone surfaces make for classic Hill Country views. You can read all about the area and its importance on signage outside the visitor center, then head to the Backcountry Trailhead where an informational sign with a map and a bench mark the beginning of Joe Johnston Route.

Right away you will notice Ashe juniper, Texas persimmon, Texas mountain laurel, honey mesquite, and cedar elm, plus an occasional live oak lining the wide, level dirt-and-gravel trail. Break out your hat, because from the start the hike is open and sunny with only brief sections of partial shade depending on the time of day.

You'll continue on this path, which is intermittently gravel and packed dirt with an almost imperceptible incline, for 2.9 miles. Regular trail markers confirm that you are still on Joe Johnston Route and inform you how many miles you have to go before you reach the famed dino tracks.

In spring and summer, you can spot various wildflowers along the trail, but watch out for poison ivy, too. In late fall, several deciduous trees, including cedar elm, bring some color to the park and you may spot a bit of yellow, orange, and red.

At 2.6 miles, you'll arrive at the dinosaur tracks left in flat, usually dried-up limestone creek beds at the base of a cliff (where you'll be headed shortly). Wander around and see if you can spot all of the tracks in this lush riparian zone before you continue on Joe Johnston Route through elegant live oak trees draped with Spanish moss.

When you turn left onto Overlook Trail, the historic Zizelman house on your right, you'll transition to a narrower and partially shaded rocky dirt path flanked by Texas

A view from the overlook at the highest point of the trail.

persimmon, Ashe juniper, and agarita and start to ascend. The hike up to the overlook isn't steep, but it is rocky in places with several large step-ups on chunky limestone boulders. When you arrive at the overlook, gaze over the lip of the cliff to spot the dinosaur tracks directly below.

Continue on, then veer left onto Caroline's Loop, which you'll be on briefly before curving right to return to Joe Johnston Route. From here, retrace your steps from the first 2.3 miles of the hike to return to the trailhead.

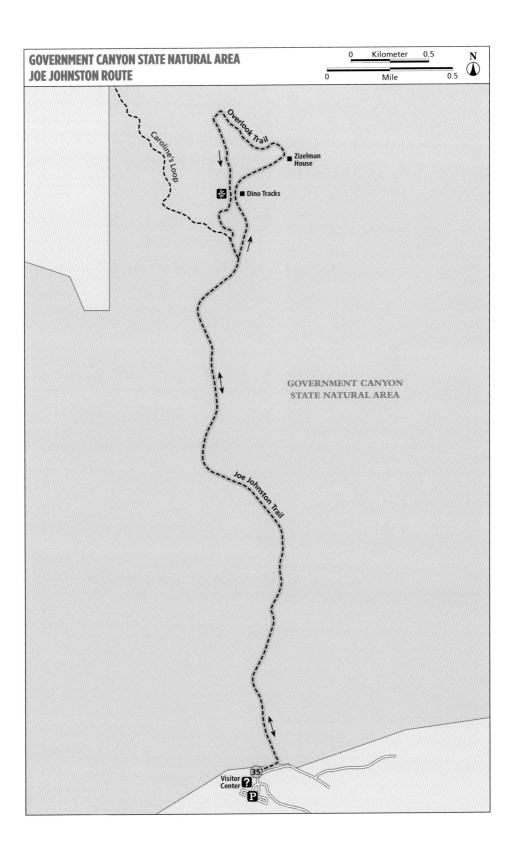

0   Kilometer   0.5

0   Mile   0.5

N

Caroline's Loop

Overlook Trail

Zizelman House

Dino Tracks

GOVERNMENT CANYON
STATE NATURAL AREA

Joe Johnston Trail

35

Visitor
Center

P

Left: Much of the trail is wide, flat, and in full sun.
Right: A portion of the trail winds through partially shaded woods.

MILES AND DIRECTIONS

0.0 Start from the Backcountry Trailhead.

0.1 Continue straight on Joe Johnston Route at the intersection with Recharge Trail.

0.9 Continue straight onto Joe Johnston at the junction with Wildcat Canyon Trail.

2.1 Continue straight on Joe Johnston at the junction with Twin Oaks Trail.

2.3 Continue straight on Joe Johnston Route past the Overlook Trail junction.

2.6 Arrive at the dinosaur tracks. Continue straight on Joe Johnston.

2.9 Turn left onto the Overlook Trail.

3.7 Arrive at the overlook.

3.9 Veer left onto Caroline's Loop.

4.0 Turn right onto Joe Johnston Route. Retrace your steps to the trailhead.

6.3 Arrive back at the trailhead. Make your way back to the visitor center and parking lot.

36 GOVERNMENT CANYON STATE NATURAL AREA BLUFF SPURS TRAIL

Stunning overlooks, a variety of scenery and plant life, and plentiful shaded sections make this moderately challenging hike a true pleasure to traverse. You'll trek through sunny plateaus peppered with cacti and persimmon, through shady Ashe juniper groves, and among wildflowers and yucca. But the multiple epic viewpoints are the highlight of this trail, made even more spectacular if you can time your hike just right to catch sunset over Hill Country.

Start: The Backcountry Trailhead
Elevation gain: 1,020 to 1,212 feet
Distance: 4.1-mile lollipop
Difficulty: Moderate due to several sections of rocky inclines and rough, uneven trail
Hiking time: 2 hours
Seasons/schedule: Year-round, Fri–Mon 7 a.m.–10 p.m., closed Tues–Thurs
Fees and permits: Day-use fee 13+ $6, children 12 and under free
Trail contacts: Government Canyon State Natural Area, 12861 Galm Rd., San Antonio, TX 78254; (210) 688-9055; https://tpwd.texas.gov/state-parks/government-canyon
Canine compatibility: No pets allowed
Trail surface: Gravel, dirt, rock

Land status: Texas Parks and Wildlife Department
Nearest town: San Antonio
Other trail users: Mountain bikers (Recharge Trail only)
Maps: Texas Parks and Wildlife Department, https://tpwd.texas.gov/publications/pwdpubs/media/park_maps/pwd_mp_p4505_0165e.pdf
Water availability: Yes, at visitor center
Special considerations: Sunsets are lovely from the overlooks, but don't forget a headlamp if you plan to hike in the dark.
Amenities available: Restrooms, benches, shelter located at visitor center
Maximum grade: 10% for 0.8 miles
Cell service: Cell service throughout

FINDING THE TRAILHEAD

From the visitor center, walk alongside the building down the cement walkway toward the asphalt trail. Cross the bridge on the sidewalk to get to the Backcountry Trailhead, which is 0.1 miles from the visitor center. Signage will guide the way. **GPS:** 29.550056, -98.762597

Trail conditions: There are some sections of smooth, packed dirt trail, but it is largely uneven and rocky. Approximately half of the trail is in full sun, the other half in partial shade.

THE HIKE

The presence of dinosaur tracks isn't the only thing that makes Government Canyon State Natural Area unique (Hike 35): It's also part of the Edwards Aquifer, Hill Country's beloved karst aquifer (it stretches across thirteen counties and covers approximately 5,400 square miles), which is characterized by caves, sinkholes, and underground streams.

A rocky trail in the later afternoon sun.

This natural area is only open Friday to Monday. The park is used for research Tuesday to Thursday. Many trails also close after heavy rains, so check with the park about trail conditions before you arrive. Reservations are recommended.

Top: Sunset from one of the west-facing overlooks.
Bottom: A wide, sunny dirt path curves through low plant life for a portion of the route.

Left: A sunny view from one of the overlooks.
Right: The rocky trail is frequently in at least partial shade.

As a result, you'll spot plenty of classic limestone rock features and area plant life like prickly pear cactus, Texas persimmon, Ashe juniper, Texas mountain laurel, and native grasses. In the spring, bright yellow cactus blooms color the trail, and in the fall, a variety of trees bring a smattering of warm hues to the landscape.

Begin on Joe Johnston Route at the Backcountry Trailhead. It's a wide gravel path, but you'll soon turn onto Recharge Trail and hike gradually up an uneven and rocky path. You'll be in full sun at this point, but several sections of extended partial shade throughout the trail break up fully exposed stretches.

When you turn left onto Bluff Spurs Trail, you'll enter a shaded forest with live oaks and juniper. Here, the gray and white pocked and weathered limestone, blackish soil, bright green juniper, and shaggy brown bark make for a picturesque landscape.

Along this section, two out-and-back side trails to overlooks branch off: The South Spur Overlook and the North Spur Overlook. Both feature expansive views of miles and miles of canyons and hills covered in the forest green of Ashe juniper and the more muted sage of live oak, the foreground decorated with mountain laurel and Texas sotol. Sunset is a lovely time to try to plan a hike to the lookouts, which face west, but don't forget a headlamp if you plan to hike after the sun goes down.

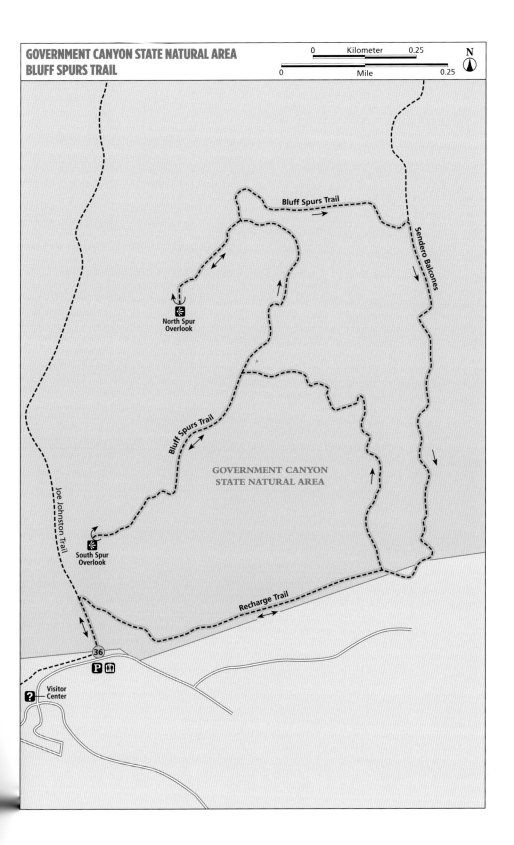

Kilometer

0   0.25

Mile

0   0.25

N

Bluff Spurs Trail

Sendero Balcones

North Spur
Overlook

Bluff Spurs Trail

GOVERNMENT CANYON
STATE NATURAL AREA

South Spur
Overlook

Joe Johnston Trail

Recharge Trail

36

P

Visitor
Center

Once you've enjoyed the view at both viewpoints, you can turn around and retrace your steps, but continuing onto Sendero Balcones is only 0.1 miles longer and offers an entirely different hiking experience, so is recommended.

Sendero Balcones will lead you back downhill, sometimes on a narrow and close wooded trail, sometimes on wide-open, sunny, and rocky paths. Follow it until you run into Recharge Trail, which will take you to Joe Johnston Route and back to the trailhead.

MILES AND DIRECTIONS

0.0   Start from the Backcountry Trailhead.

0.1   Turn right onto Recharge Trail.

0.6   Turn left onto Bluff Spurs Trail.

1.1   Veer left at the junction with South Spur Overlook trail.

1.5   Reach the South Spur Overlook. Turn around and retrace your steps to the last junction.

1.9   Continue straight at the junction with Bluff Spurs Trail following signs for the main loop.

2.2   Curve slightly left to the North Spur Overlook. Signs will guide your way.

2.4   Reach the North Spur Overlook. Turn around and retrace your steps to the last junction.

2.6   Turn left to continue on Bluff Spurs Trail.

2.9   Turn right onto Sendero Balcones Trail.

3.5   Turn right onto Recharge Trail following signs for the parking lot.

3.5   Follow the main trail as it curves to the right, passing the campground access trail.

3.6   Continue straight on Recharge Trail.

3.9   Follow Recharge Trail as it curves to the right.

4.0   Turn left onto Joe Johnston Route.

4.1   Arrive back at the trailhead.

37 HILL COUNTRY STATE NATURAL AREA WEST PEAK OVERLOOK TRAIL

There are few trails with such expansive and impressive views of Hill Country as West Peak Overlook Trail. A delightful hike on its own, it can also be linked to several other trails if you have a longer route around the park in mind. And though not always the case with an overlook trail, this one offers views that are more than worth the exceedingly rocky and often steep climb.

Start: The Merrick Mile Trailhead
Elevation gain: 1,508 to 1,893 feet
Distance: 3.0-mile lollipop
Difficulty: Moderate due to rocky terrain and elevation gain
Hiking time: 2 hours
Seasons/schedule: Year-round but best enjoyed fall through spring; park office hours are 8:15 a.m.–4:45 p.m.
Fees and permits: Day-use fee 13+ $6, children under 12 free
Trail contacts: Texas State Parks, Hill Country Natural Area, 10600 Bandera Creek Rd., Bandera, TX 78003; (830) 796-4413; https://tpwd.texas.gov/state-parks/hill-country
Canine compatibility: On-leash only
Trail surface: Dirt, rock
Land status: Texas Parks and Wildlife

Nearest town: Bandera
Other trail users: Horses, mountain bikers
Maps: Texas Parks and Wildlife, https://tpwd.texas.gov/publications/pwdpubs/media/park_maps/pwd_mp_p4507_0115g.pdf
Water availability: Yes, near the visitor center
Special considerations: Most of this trail is in full sun, so bring sun protection and plenty of water, especially in warmer months.
Amenities available: Restrooms near visitor center, benches on shaded porch
Maximum grade: 12% for 0.8 miles
Cell service: Some service near visitor center (including Wi-Fi) but spotty along trail

FINDING THE TRAILHEAD

Park in the gravel lot near the visitor center. A metal trail marker that signifies the beginning of Merrick Mile Trail with be toward the northwest end of the parking loop. **GPS:** 29.628024, -99.182187

Trail conditions: The trail is both smooth packed dirt and uneven and rocky at times, with the latter being the more common. Most of the trail is in full sun, so it can be brutally hot in the summer.

THE HIKE

Hill Country State Natural Area, and this hike in particular, feels like the quintessential Hill Country experience: open prairie, tall grasses, wildflowers in the spring, an abundance of live oak and juniper, plus plenty of yucca and Texas sotol line the trail throughout the hike. Bushy and bright evergreen sumac, hearty agarita, and delicate yellow damianita flowers offer plenty of vibrant color to balance the bright blue skies and ubiquitous white limestone.

The rocky trail leading to the overlook flanked by yucca and other native plants.

A bench at one of the overlooks.

Start your hike on the wide and dusty path in open prairie surrounded by plant life and possibly horses—the park is popular among trail riders. But don't worry, if you find flat dirt paths less than exhilarating, you'll soon reach the uneven, rocky uphill sections that remind you why it's called Hill Country.

The most strenuous section of prolonged uphill starts at 0.6 miles, just after veering onto West Peak Overlook Trail, and continues for nearly a mile. The rocks are loose and uneven in places, so take your time as you ascend.

Fortunately, along the way are plenty of places to stop and enjoy the view. You'll even spot a bench or two at the top of strenuous climbs where you can catch your breath while you gaze out over the surrounding hills. In fact, the landscape surrounding the park is about as hilly as Hill Country gets, making the park aptly named.

Continue on West Peak Overlook Trail until you reach the very top of the hill and an open space with a bench and an informational sign. This is where the overlook loop begins, which offers stunning views from nearly every direction. Take a hard left to stay on West Peak Overlook Trail. The narrow trail will continue up. As you ascend, several side trails will branch off from time to time, but stay on the steep rocky path.

As you approach the main overlook, prickly pear cactus will make an appearance alongside the narrow, rocky way and provide a picturesque foreground for views of the

> Several times a year Texas State Natural Areas are open only for hunting and are closed for hiking for several days. Trails and backcountry campsites may also close due to wet conditions or poor weather. Check the park website before you go.

A sunny trail near the peak.

valley below and the peaks beyond when you finally reach the overlook at 1,868 feet (there's an elevation marker). Take a break after the long climb and enjoy the expansive view.

When you're ready to continue, complete the overlook loop and when you return to the first junction with Spring Branch Trail, start heading back down the mountain the way you came.

HILL COUNTRY STATE NATURAL AREA WEST PEAK OVERLOOK TRAIL

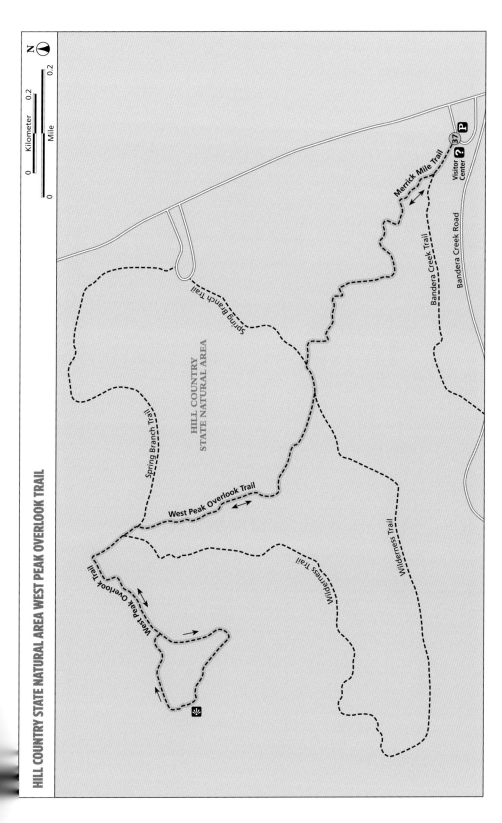

The view from one of the overlooks.

MILES AND DIRECTIONS

0.0 Start from Merrick Mile Trailhead.

0.1 Continue straight on Merrick Mile at the intersection with Bandera Creek Trail.

0.5 Continue straight onto West Peak Overlook Trail.

0.6 Veer left to continue on West Peak Overlook/Wilderness Trail. Then veer right to stay on West Peak Overlook Trail.

1.0 Continue straight on West Peak Overlook as you pass Spring Branch Trail on your right, then left.

1.1 Take a hard left to stay on West Peak Overlook Trail.

1.3 Arrive at an overlook.

1.5 Arrive at West Peak Overlook.

1.8 Complete the overlook loop. Head back the way you came.

1.9 Turn right at the intersection with Spring Branch Trail to head back down the hill on West Peak Overlook Trail.

2.0 Continue straight on West Peak Overlook Trail past two junctions with Spring Branch Trail.

2.5 Veer left to stay on West Peak Overlook/Wilderness Trail. Veer right to continue on Merrick Mile.

2.9 Continue straight across Bandera Creek Trail.

3.0 Arrive back at the trailhead parking lot.

38 HILL COUNTRY STATE NATURAL AREA COUGAR CANYON OVERLOOK TRAIL

Some of the most remote regions of this state natural area are also the most picturesque. And this trail will lead you there. While this route is beloved by rangers, the multitude of looping trails that branch off along the route offer the option to choose your own adventure, adding or subtracting miles at your leisure. But while this trail may be long and sunny with sections of steep, rocky climbs, the views offer a worthy payoff (and each shaded section feels all the sweeter).

Start: The Spring Branch Trail Trailhead on the north end of the Equestrian Camp Area parking lot
Elevation gain: 1,536 to 1,930 feet
Distance: 7.3-mile loop
Difficulty: Moderate due to rocky terrain and elevation gain
Hiking time: 3.5 hours
Seasons/schedule: Year-round but best enjoyed fall through spring
Fees and permits: Day-use fee 13+ $6, children under 12 free
Trail contacts: Texas State Parks, Hill Country Natural Area, 10600 Bandera Creek Rd., Bandera, TX 78003; (830) 796-4413; https://tpwd.texas.gov/state-parks/hill-country
Canine compatibility: On-leash only
Trail surface: Dirt, rock

Land status: Texas Parks and Wildlife
Nearest town: Bandera
Other trail users: Horses, mountain bikers
Maps: Texas Parks and Wildlife, https://tpwd.texas.gov/publications/pwdpubs/media/park_maps/pwd_mp_p4507_0115g.pdf
Water availability: Yes
Special considerations: Much of this trail is in full sun, so bring sun protection and plenty of water in warmer months.
Amenities available: Restrooms at trailhead
Maximum grade: 13% for 0.3 miles
Cell service: Some service near visitor center (including Wi-Fi) but spotty along trail

FINDING THE TRAILHEAD

Drive past the visitor center on the gravel park road. The first gravel lot on your left is the equestrian camp parking area and trailhead. The trailhead itself splits off the wide dirt path on the north side of the lot. **GPS:** 29.634501, -99.184476

Trail conditions: The trail transitions between packed dirt and uneven, rocky surfaces. Most of the trail is in full sun with sections of partial shade.

THE HIKE

This winding path has it all: sun, shade, flat prairies, rocky climbs, views, and plenty of plant life. You have the option to make the hike longer or shorter to suit as plenty of trails intersect along the way.

Start your hike in the morning to avoid trekking in the hottest part of the day. Morning or evening, listen for the rustling of armadillos digging for their dinner in the dirt and leaves or watch for white tailed deer among the juniper. Whether or not you spot wildlife, you're sure to witness plenty of Texas flora, from shrubby persimmon trees and the occasional live oak to tiny yellow gummed flowers and yucca.

A rocky path surrounded by native plant life.

A wide section of trail through the prairie.

As you begin, a narrow dirt path will lead you down a juniper-lined trail. The trail will follow alongside the gravel roadway for 0.2 miles before veering off to the left where it becomes rocky and begins to climb gradually.

At 0.7 miles, the trail overlaps for a moment with the West Peak Overlook Trail, which is a recommended addition to your route if you haven't completed Hike 29 yet. Otherwise, continue on Spring Branch Trail where you'll be treated to a few brief moments of partial shade.

Once you reach the top of the climb, head downhill almost immediately on a rocky trail with some sections of large step-downs and enjoy more sections of partial shade as you enter forests of juniper, live oak, Mexican buckeye, and madrone.

Once you turn onto Madrone Trail, you'll head back up and pop out onto a sunny dirt path wide enough for two. Half a mile later you'll pass an old house at the top of the hill and continue on Madrone until you reach Cougar Canyon Overlook Trail, where you'll turn left and start ascending.

The climb up from this point is steep and rugged, but don't forget to turn around to enjoy the frequent vistas colored with prickly pear cactus and wildflowers. The official overlook is at 4.3 miles, where, if there's been sufficient rain recently, you'll get a long view of the creek bed in the valley below just before you descend a steep, rocky slope.

Several times a year Texas State Natural Areas are open only for hunting and are closed for hiking for several days. Check the website before you go to make sure you're not visiting during an open hunt. Reservations are recommended on weekends and holidays and check the park website before you go to make sure trails aren't closed due to weather.

Yucca along the trail.

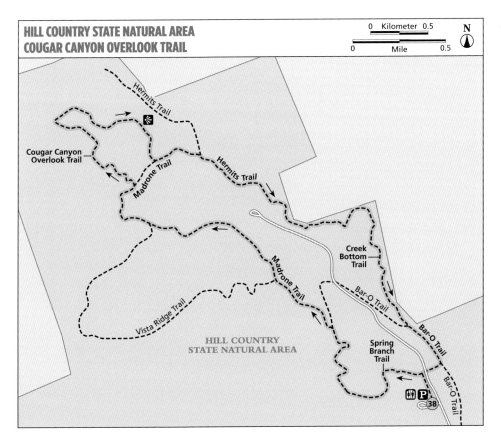

At the bottom of the descent, continue through sections of woods and grassland as you transition to Hermits Trail, where the trail becomes wider and smoother, followed by Creek Bottom Trail, a sometimes wide, fairly washed-out path.

You'll cross a handful of creek beds that will often be dry except after significant rainfall and transition to Bar-O Trail and a final section of prairie where tall, golden grasses bow to the breeze.

When the trail runs into the gravel park road, cross and continue to the other side where you will turn left to take Spring Branch Trail back toward the trailhead as you retrace your steps from the first 0.2 miles of your hike.

MILES AND DIRECTIONS

0.0 Start at Spring Branch Trailhead.

0.2 Turn left to stay on Spring Branch Trail.

0.7 Continue straight as the trail overlaps momentarily with the West Peak Overlook Trail.

0.8 Turn right onto Spring Branch Trail.

1.0 Continue on Spring Branch Trail.

1.3 Turn left onto Madrone Trail

A wide, sunny path with big views.

1.7 Veer right by the old house at the top of the hill to continue on Madrone Trail.

1.8 Turn left to stay on Madrone Trail.

2.6 Continue straight to stay on Madrone Trail at the junction with Vista Ridge Trail.

3.0 Turn left onto Cougar Canyon Overlook Trail.

4.3 Reach the overlook.

4.6 Turn left onto Madrone Trail.

4.8 Turn right onto Hermits Trail.

5.1 Veer left to stay on Hermits Trail.

5.2 Continue straight to stay on Hermits Trail.

5.8 Continue straight onto Creek Bottom Trail at the junction with Hermits Trail.

6.2 Turn left onto Creek Bottom Trail. When the trail looks like splits again in a few more steps, continue to the right.

6.6 Cross a (usually) dry creek bed.

6.8 Cross another (usually) dry creek bed. Turn left onto Bar-O Trail.

7.0 Continue straight on Bar-O Trail.

7.1 Veer right at the Y-junction through the prairie.

7.2 Cross the gravel park road and turn left onto Spring Branch Trail on the other side. Retrace your steps from the first 0.2 miles of the hike.

7.4 Arrive back at the trailhead parking lot.

39 GARNER STATE PARK OL' BALDY

This strenuous hike may be tricky to follow at times, require scrambling over steep sections of rock, and experience full sun for most of the day, but the views, plant life, and diversity of terrain are disproportionally epic to the actual length of the hike, meaning you'll get serious bang for your buck on every mile. You can cut the trail in half by completing a simple out-and-back to the summit, but then you'll miss the vista of Ol' Baldy itself and the valleys that flank either side. Just make sure to bring plenty of water, your camera, and a sense of adventure.

Start: The Ol' Baldy/White Rock Cave Trail Trailhead
Elevation gain: 1,391 to 1,854 feet
Distance: 2.1-mile loop
Difficulty: Difficult due to numerous steep and rocky inclines
Hiking time: 2 hours
Seasons/schedule: Year-round, 8 a.m.–10 p.m.
Fees and permits: Day-use fee 13+ $8, 12 and under free
Trail contacts: Garner State Park, 234 RR 1050, Concan, TX 78838; (830) 232-6132; https://tpwd.texas .gov/state-parks/garner
Canine compatibility: On-leash only

Trail surface: Dirt, rock
Land status: Texas State Park
Nearest town: Rio Frio (unincorporated)
Other trail users: Hikers only
Maps: Texas State Parks, https:// tpwd.texas.gov/publications/pwd pubs/media/park_maps/pwd_mp _p4507_0061q.pdf
Water availability: Yes
Special considerations: Most of this trail is in full sun and can be brutally hot in the summer. Plan accordingly.
Amenities available: Restrooms
Maximum grade: 20% for 0.5 miles
Cell service: Throughout

FINDING THE TRAILHEAD

From the main entrance, follow signs for the Park Store and Pecan Grove Camping Area. The trailhead parking lot is located on the left side of the park road just 0.2 miles past the Park Store (there's more parking down the road at the Garner State Park Store). The trailhead is on the right. **GPS:** 29.579887, -99.733471

Trail conditions: Much of this trail is in full sun, though there are a few sections of partial shade. There are many sections of very steep and rocky inclines that may require scrambling.

THE HIKE

Garner State Park may be most popular in the summer when tubing, kayaking, and swimming in the sparkling Frio River offer a refreshing respite from the summer heat, but the hikes and views available year-round make this a park worth visiting any time of year.

In the spring, you're likely to spot wildflowers. In the fall, cypress trees along the river bring a warm hue to the landscape. And in the winter, junipers and other evergreens keep the trails lively and welcoming.

A sunny path with a view leads to Ol' Baldy.

And of all the hikes in the 1,174-acre park, Ol' Baldy may be the most rewarding when it comes to views. After all, the summit is the highest point in the park. And after the short but challenging hike, there are plenty of ways to enjoy the rest of your day or weekend: hike more of the 16 miles of trails, lounge in a tube in the river, visit the ice cream shop or pollinator garden, or camp for a night or two.

As soon as you begin, you'll be surrounded by Texas mountain laurel, juniper, and oak trees. Soapberry, Buckley's oak, yucca, and lots of greenery colors the trail and offers respites of shade from time to time. Just a few steps in, keep left at the fork, following metal signposts for Ol' Baldy.

A narrow dirt path strewn with rocks is marked with a yellow footprint but quickly starts to climb up a rocky, uneven slope. Much of the trail at this point will be in full sun during midday, and there is lots of loose rock, so take care as you plant your feet and bring sun protection. The trail can be difficult to follow at times, but keep an eye out for the yellow footprints for confirmation you're on the right path.

Once you reach the top of the steep climb, the trail levels out a bit and you will find slightly more shade thanks to Ashe juniper, oaks, and persimmon. Honey mesquite and prickly pear cactus also flank trails as you gain elevation. But it's those rocky hills and trails, plus plenty of opportunities for photo ops of the valley below and that keep the hike interesting.

At the first major intersection with Foshee Trail, turn left to continue to the Ol' Baldy summit. A map and signage will guide the way. When you reach the summit area after another brief but steep ascent, an extended loop allows you to circumnavigate the top and take in views from every side.

The rocky trail is frequently surrounded by plants like yucca and juniper.

The afternoon sun shines through the trees near the summit.

This park is extremely popular on summer weekends, so reservations are encouraged and often required.

A view of the winding river and surrounding hills from near the summit.

Arrive back at the last junction and veer left to continue down Foshee Trail. When you come to the signposted Old Rock Fence, turn left. Shortly after, a jumble of trails intersect. Turn right to follow signs for Bird Trail, which turns into White Rock Cave Trail. Continue to follow the yellow footprints painted on the ground as you wend and scramble over steep sections of large rocks.

When you reach White Rock Cave, take a peek inside the small cave before continuing on your way down one more steep, rocky section that leads you back down to the trailhead.

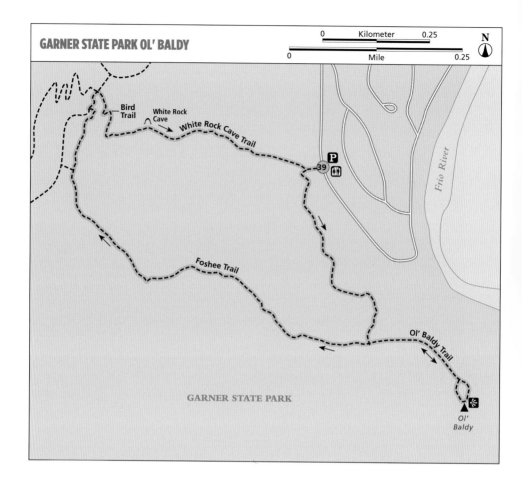

MILES AND DIRECTIONS

0.0   Start from Ol' Baldy Trailhead. Keep left at the fork following metal signposts for Ol' Baldy.

0.4   Veer left at the junction with Ol' Baldy and Foshee Trail to continue to the summit.

0.5   Reach the summit area.

0.7   Retrace your steps back to the last junction.

0.9   At the junction with Ol' Baldy and Foshee Trail veer onto Foshee Trail.

1.5   Turn left to proceed onto Foshee through the opening in a low rock fence (Old Rock Fence).

1.6   At an intersection with several trails, turn right following signs for Bird Trail.

1.7   Arrive at White Rock Cave.

1.9   At an unmarked junction, turn right to continue down the steep rocky trail.

2.1   Arrive back at the trailhead.

40 GARNER STATE PARK CRYSTAL CAVE TRAIL

Gradual inclines, a shaded cave, picturesque overlooks, and the sounds of water running in the riverbed below make this trail a delightfully short but sweet hike in a state park that's popular for its swimming holes in the summer and fall foliage in autumn. And if you're paying the park a visit, this trail shouldn't be missed. It can even be lengthened by tacking on a trek to Ol' Baldy if you'd like to extend your excursion and tackle a handful of trails in one go.

Start: The Madrone Walkway Trailhead
Elevation gain: 1,376 to 1,798 feet
Distance: 1.4-mile lollipop
Difficulty: Moderate due to prolonged gradual inclines and uneven trail surfaces
Hiking time: 1.5 hours
Seasons/schedule: Year-round, 8 a.m.–10 p.m.
Fees and permits: Day-use fee 13+ $8, 12 and under free
Trail contacts: Garner State Park, 234 RR 1050, Concan, TX 78838; (830) 232-6132; https://tpwd.texas .gov/state-parks/garner
Canine compatibility: On-leash only
Trail surface: Dirt, rock
Land status: Texas State Park

Nearest town: Rio Frio (unincorporated)
Other trail users: Bikers allowed on first and last 0.1 miles of paved path, then hikers only
Maps: Texas State Parks, https:// tpwd.texas.gov/publications/pwd pubs/media/park_maps/pwd_mp _p4507_0061q.pdf
Water availability: Yes
Special considerations: Bring plenty of water when hiking midday in the summer as the uphill portion sees more sun in the afternoon.
Amenities available: Restrooms, picnic tables, park store
Maximum grade: 15% for 0.8 miles
Cell service: Throughout

FINDING THE TRAILHEAD

From the main entrance, follow signs for the Gift Shop and Pavilion. A parking lot will be located on the left side of the park road near Garner Grill and the mini golf course. The trailhead is located behind the pavilion at the end of the building farthest from the parking lot. **GPS:** 29.585222, -99.734017

Trail conditions: Partial shade with both packed dirt and uneven rocky trails. A few brief sections of scrambling are required.

THE HIKE

While the summit of Ol' Baldy may be the recipient of most of the foot traffic and fan-fare when it comes to hiking in Garner State Park, this loop that leads you up hills and

> Plenty of camping is available in Garner State Park should you wish to spend the night. But consider making a reservation for camping or day use in advance in the summer when the park is popular for swimming and tubing.

Rock cairns near the highest point of the trail are stacked in front of sweeping views of Hill Country.

into caves also comes highly recommended by park rangers. The upside to the less iconic hike is that you're also less likely to find the trails crowded, even on weekends.

That could also be due to the level of exertion required to complete this hike. While it may not be as steep or strenuous as the climb to Ol' Baldy, the sustained inclines and declines last for a solid three-quarters of the trek, so some stamina is required.

Fortunately, Ashe juniper, live oak trees, honey mesquite and Texas persimmon, plus yucca and Texas sotol, line the trail and color it year-round. The larger plant life even offers some shade, though mostly early and late in the day. But fear not: The woods are rarely dense or tall enough to obscure your view of the landscape as you climb.

The trail starts as a cement sidewalk with the Rio River below on your right. You'll pass a set of stairs that lead down to the water if you want to take a closer look; otherwise, continue on the partially shaded asphalt pathway. This portion of trail is shared with bikes, so stay alert.

When you reach the road, turn right to stay on Madrone Walkway for a few more steps before crossing the road in front of a maintenance driveway; you'll see the Crystal Cave Trail Trailhead just across the street.

From the official trailhead, the dirt path will be marked by a yellow footprint with a red dot accompanied by a green dot. Wide enough for two or three and partially shaded in sections, it offers an opportunity to stroll and chat, though the rocky and uneven trail will start leading you uphill in short order and may put a strain on conversation.

Fortunately, the higher you climb, the more views you can expect as the tree cover opens up and offers views of the hills throughout the park.

At just under the halfway point, you'll arrive at Crystal Cave. Head down about 30 feet into the earth to explore, and make sure to bring your headlamp.

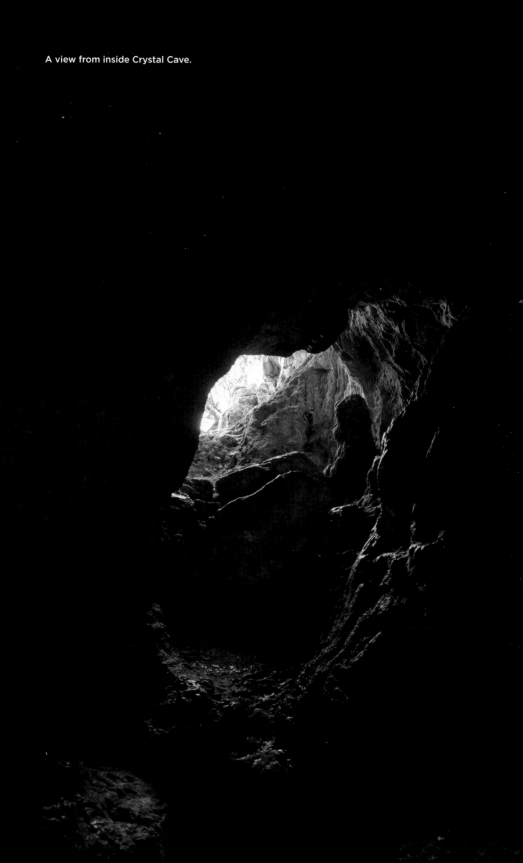

A view from inside Crystal Cave.

A rocky path leads up toward the cave.

GARNER STATE PARK CRYSTAL CAVE TRAIL

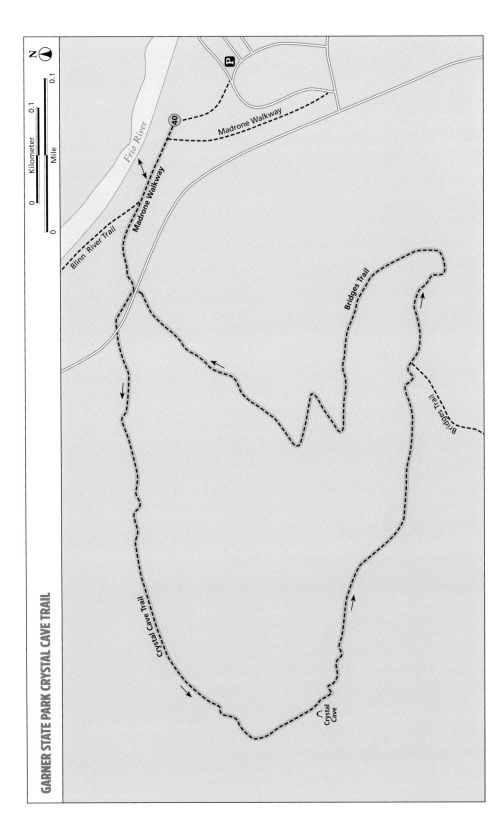

The rocky trail is occasionally in partial shade.

In about 0.2 miles, pay attention to the yellow footprints as the trail can be tricky to follow in places. When you reach the top of the hill, for example, veer left to stay on the trail. In a few more steps, turn left to transition to Bridges Trail. Here, there is a wooden sign pointing the way and you can spot Ol' Baldy straight ahead.

Begin your descent on the oversized limestone rocks; red painted dots mark the way. Once you reach the bottom of the steep decline, the trail veers left, then soon becomes a gradually curving dirt and gravel path.

When you arrive at the Bridges Trail Trailhead, cross the road and return to Madrone Walkway. Retrace your steps from the first 0.1 miles of the hike to return to the pavilion and the parking lot.

MILES AND DIRECTIONS

0.0 Start from the Madrone Walkway trailhead behind the pavilion.

0.1 Continue straight on Madrone Walkway past Blinn River Trail. Turn right at the road to stay on Madrone Walkway for a few steps, then cross the road to start on Crystal Cave Trail via the trailhead.

0.6 Arrive at Crystal Cave.

0.8 Continue on the trail as it curves left. Turn left on Bridges Trail.

0.9 Reach an overlook. Continue on the trail on the right of the informational sign. At the bottom of the descent, turn left to stay on Bridges Trail.

1.3 Arrive at the Bridges Trail Trailhead. Continue straight across the road to return to Madrone Walkway.

1.4 Arrive back at the trailhead and pavilion.

41 LOST MAPLES STATE NATURAL AREA EAST AND WEST TRAILS

Rugged terrain, cool creeks, towering limestone cliffs, swimming holes, and epic views make this strenuous and often hot hike a hit with visitors and locals alike. And while it's beautiful year-round, late fall is when the park really shines as the leaves from the many big-tooth maples for which the park is named turn from green to vibrant red in a fiery display. No matter when you visit, you're in for a treat: challenging terrain, big views, and pops of color all await in this Hill Country park.

Start: The East Trail Trailhead
Elevation gain: 1,796 to 2,270 feet
Distance: 8.1-mile loop
Difficulty: Difficult due to sun, length, and extended stretches of steep and rocky terrain
Hiking time: 4.5 hours
Seasons/schedule: Year-round but popular in the fall for autumn colors; visitor center open daily, 8 a.m.–4:30 p.m. (hiking allowed after the visitor center closes)
Fees and permits: Day-use fee 13+ $6, children 12 and under free
Trail contacts: Lost Maples State Natural Area, 37221 FM 187, Vanderpool, TX 78885; (830) 966-3413; https://tpwd.texas.gov/state -parks/lost-maples
Canine compatibility: On-leash only
Trail surface: Dirt, rock
Land status: Texas Parks and Wildlife Department

Nearest town: Utopia
Other trail users: Hikers only for most of the trail, but first sections are also open to mountain bikers
Maps: Texas Parks and Wildlife Department, https://tpwd.texas.gov/ publications/pwdpubs/media/park _maps/pwd_mp_p4507_0074g .pdf
Water availability: At trailhead
Special considerations: Much of the trail is in full sun and can get extremely hot in the summer. Bring plenty of water and sun protection.
Amenities available: Restrooms, picnic tables, shelters, drinking fountain
Maximum grade: 20% for 0.4 miles
Cell service: Spotty cell service usually only available at high points; not available in the parking areas

FINDING THE TRAILHEAD

 From the park entrance, take the park road to the main parking lot at the East Trailhead. The trail begins at the very end of the lot. There is an overflow parking lot just up the park road by the East-West Trailhead.
GPS: 29.816779, -99.570920

Trail conditions: The trail is occasionally flat and smooth packed dirt or crushed granite, but more often it is rocky and uneven with several very steep sections. Most of East Trail is in full sun.

THE HIKE

Named for the area's towering bigtooth maples, this natural area is a marvel and a wonder, and extremely popular with hikers and backpackers across Texas. High limestone cliffs, low valleys, creeks and swimming holes make it inviting year-round, but it's the maples

In the fall, vibrant leaves color the trail.

The park often fills to capacity on weekends and every day in the fall. Advance reservations are highly recommended as the park will not admit new visitors after it has reached capacity. Frontcountry and backcountry camping are available in the park.

The pond near the midway point offers a delightful place to take a dip or enjoy a rest.

that make it an extra special attraction in October and November when leaves begin to turn deep red.

As a result, on weekends (and daily in the fall) the park is often full to capacity. Fortunately, even on fall weekends, most hikers stick to East Trail and East-West Trail, so for the rest of the hike you may be able to enjoy a quieter experience.

Begin at the East Trail Trailhead at the far end of the parking lot and day-use area. A sign will guide you down the gravel path lined with large boulders and blazed with

A rocky walkway flanked by trees.

green arrows and flanked by plants like Texas mountain laurel, juniper, and Texas persimmon, plus prairie flameleaf sumac. Twist leaf yucca, the occasional madrone, and Mexican buckeye can be spotted trailside, too, and together the foliage offers partial shade during the first part of the hike.

You'll pass creeks (which will often be dry except during seasons of heavy rain) and wide-open prairies, tall grasses and riparian zones, and limestone cliffs and hollowed-out grottos, the most notable being Monkey Rock, which is accessible via a short side trail that leads you to the creek and the aptly named limestone structure. Follow the signs to dip your toes and snap a photo.

At 1.6 miles, the picturesque grotto surrounded by ferns and other vibrant greenery marks the start of the first steep, rocky climb with several sections of large step-ups. The trail only gets more rugged from here and will be in full sun for many miles.

After you reach the top, turn left to stroll down the rocky but level path to the overlook that offers wide views of the valley, cliffs, and hills beyond and below. This side trail will add 0.7 miles to your hike round-trip but is flat and easy. Several more overlooks follow.

When you reach the side trail for primitive camping area B, it's time to head back down into the valley. This steep section is uneven with lots of loose rock, large step-downs, and little shade. But once you reach the bottom of the hill, you'll be rewarded with a pond that makes a great swimming hole in warmer months. There are plenty of shady spots to sit and rest, including at picnic tables. A drop toilet is also available. Continue onto West Trail, which is marked with blue arrows.

From here, expect intermittent sun and partial shade, creek bed crossings, and walking across limestone outcroppings on the low cliffs and uneven bottom of what might have once been a creek bed, all surrounded by more riparian plant life.

Finally, near 7.5 miles, you'll cross a running creek on large steppingstones and veer right onto East-West Trail following signs for trailhead parking. After another crossing a few minutes later, East-West Trail ends on the park road just below the overflow parking lot. If you parked in the day-use area, continue straight down the park road following signs for the day-use/picnic area and follow signs for "trail to day-use area." It will spit you back out into the day-use parking lot.

A sunny gravel path weaves through a prairie and by colorful maples.

LOST MAPLES STATE NATURAL AREA EAST AND WEST TRAILS

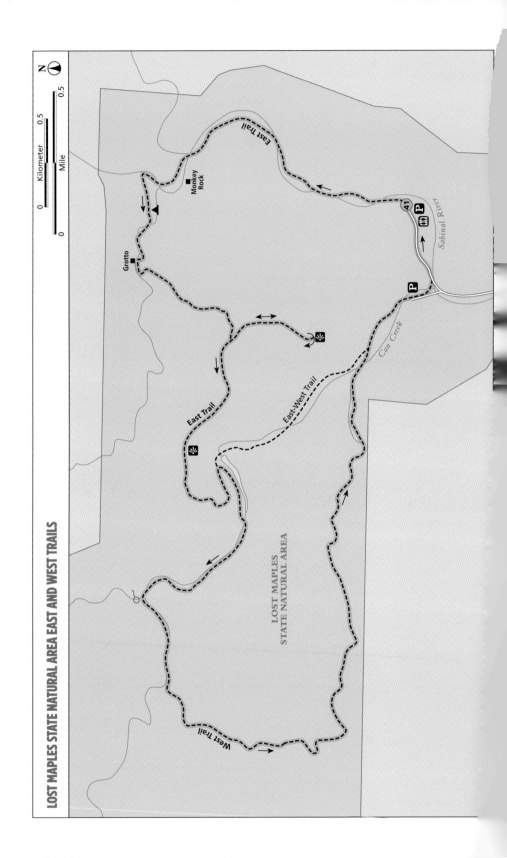

MILES AND DIRECTIONS

0.0 Start from East Trail Trailhead. After a few steps the trail splits but reconnects in 0.5 miles. Veer right to stay on the wide gravel path.

1.1 Turn left at the sign for Monkey Rock to take a short detour to the creek bed and Monkey Rock.

1.3 Veer left to stay on East Trail past the sign for primitive camping area A.

1.6 Arrive at the grotto.

2.2 Turn left to stay onto Overlook Trail for a 0.7-mile addition to your hike and views of the valley.

2.6 Arrive at the overlook, turn around, and retrace your steps to the junction with East Trail.

3.0 Continue straight onto East Trail.

3.6 More overlooks. Continue straight on East Trail at the junction with primitive camping area B.

3.9 Arrive at the pond. Turn right to continue onto West Trail.

4.6 Continue straight past the gravel service road.

4.7 Arrive at a natural spring.

5.1 Turn left at the junction with West Loop Trail to continue on West Trail.

Rocky trails are frequently the norm at Lost Maples.

6.0 Continue past the side trail to primitive camping area E.

6.5 Continue past primitive camping area D.

7.5 Turn right to stay on West Trail. Cross the creek and veer right onto East-West Trail following signs for trailhead parking.

7.8 Cross the creek. Exit East-West Trail just below the overflow parking lot. Continue straight down the park road following signs for day-use/picnic area.

7.9 Turn left onto the dirt path marked with a sign that says "Trail to day-use area."

8.0 Turn left onto the park road and cross the road at the crosswalk. Continue on the connector trail on the other side.

8.1 Arrive back at the day-use area and parking lot.

HIKE INDEX

THE TEN ESSENTIALS OF HIKING

American Hiking Society

American Hiking Society recommends you pack the "Ten Essentials" every time you head out for a hike. Whether you plan to be gone for a couple of hours or several months, make sure to pack these items. Become familiar with these items and know how to use them. Learn more at **AmericanHiking.org/hiking-resources**

1. Appropriate Footwear

6. Safety Items (light, fire, and a whistle)

2. Navigation

7. First Aid Kit

3. Water (and a way to purify it)

8. Knife or Multi-Tool

4. Food

9. Sun Protection

5. Rain Gear & Dry-Fast Layers

10. Shelter